The Great Canon
CONTROVERSY

WILLIAM·CASEMENT

The Great Canon
CONTROVERSY

The Battle of the Books in Higher Education

TRANSACTION PUBLISHERS
New Brunswick (U.S.A.) and London (U.K.)

This book is printed on acid-free paper that meets the American National
Standard for Permanence of Paper for Printed Library Materials.

Library of Congress Catalog Number: 95-13197
ISBN: 1-56000-276-X
Printed in the United States of America

Library of Congress Cataloging-in-Publication Data
Casement, William
The great canon controversy : the battle of the books in higher education /
William Casement. — 1st ed.
p.   cm.
Includes bibliographical references (p. 155) and index.
ISBN 1-56000-276-X (cloth)
1. Education, Higher—United States—Curricula.   2. Literature (Canon)
3. Education, Higher—Political aspects—United States.
4. Political correctness—United States.   5. Multicultural
education—United States.   I. Title.
LB2361.5.C39   1995
378.1'99'0973—dc20   95-13197
                                                                    CIP

To Christopher and Alexander,
who I hope will come to appreciate reading great books
as much as I have.

CONTENTS

PREFACE

American higher education is going through a period of intense controversy over the curriculum, and at the center of it is a dispute over teaching the "canon"—the collection of "great books" authored by Homer, Plato, Shakespeare, Kant, Darwin, and many others that has long represented the Western intellectual tradition. College faculty and administrators engage in heated discussions about the appropriateness of the canon, with students sometimes brought into the fray. And news about the controversy has reached the general public through national media coverage, with major newspapers, magazines, and television networks reporting on Stanford University's revision of its reading list.

The controversy might be thought of as the college curriculum's encounter with what some people would disparagingly call "political correctness" and other people would supportively call "multiculturalism." The great divide between these two perspectives, which view basically the same territory but from opposite directions, is reflected in discussion about the canon. On one side are defenders of the canon, who argue for the pedagogical superiority of the great books. On the other side are anticanonists, who believe that those books, and the tradition they represent, should give way to new books and an emphasis on new ways of thinking. Much rhetoric has been tossed about and much ink spilled as the main lines of argument for both sides have been staked out, along with various angles and subtleties. Occasionally, leaders from one side or the other offer signals of rapprochement, and uncommitted third parties call for resolution through compromise. But for the most part partisanship reigns, and circumspect overviews of the situation are rare.

My purpose in this book is to provide such an overview, and at the same time point toward what I believe is a sensible resolution to the controversy. My position is not nonpartisan, however, as I am a strong supporter of the canon and I believe that much of what its critics have to say is exaggerated, distorted, or simply wrong. Still, the critics should not be dismissed out of hand; their ideas deserve careful scrutiny, and when it is given, some of them will prove to be acceptable as the basis for needed canon revision.

Part I of my discussion is an historical account that traces the practice of teaching the great books from ancient Greece to the present. Many parties today—especially anticanonists, but sometimes canonists as well—pay little attention to the canon's past other than to make a few broad (often inaccurate) generalizations about it. But that past is pertinent to the present. Curriculum dispute focusing on the canon is not a new occurrence. Over the centuries there have been several major controversies, a recounting of which is helpful in understanding the stance canonists take today. Their views on what comprises a proper education and their arguments for the need to study the great books are based in ideas that have a long and important historical standing. Further, an understanding of the canon's more recent history, recent in this case meaning the last couple of centuries, will help us to appreciate that when the current struggle began, the practice of teaching the great books had long been in decline and was not a major factor in the education of most students. The anticanon movement has brought renewed attention to the canon that it could not have generated itself.

Part II summarizes the contemporary anticanon movement in terms of its epistemological and political dimensions, and their effect on the curriculum. Recent ideas in philosophy and literary theory have militated against the belief that the great books are a means for acquiring a knowledge of universal truths or values such as many canon supporters have claimed; in fact, the existence of such a knowledge at all is denied. Left-wing politics have associated the canon with political conservativism and with an exclusivist and elitist concentration on Western culture. There has been much pressure to add or substitute readings critical of traditional views concerning class, gender, race, and works from outside of Western culture. Not only are reading lists being altered, but the great books remaining on them are often treated as anything but great—as examples of outdated and politically incorrect ways of thinking.

My rebuttal addresses several of the main epistemological and political claims of anticanonism. At the heart of the matter are the principles of unity and plurality. Anticanonists tend to see plurality when they should see unity, and vice versa. Their denial of universal truths not only falters on its own logic and nearsightedness, but it undercuts the validity of the political agenda it has been allied with. On the other hand, the anticanonist claim that the great books are unified under the banner of political conservativism fails to recognize both the pluralism of the ideas to be found in those works and the fact that left-wing thinking, too, can align in favor of teaching the canon.

In spite of the defects and excesses of the anticanon movement, it stands in the right in calling for the curriculum to include certain kinds of books that have not been part of the traditional canon. Part III addresses the matter of canon revision, favoring it on a limited basis, and arguing against canonists who have opposed it. But the revision must be kept in proper perspective so that the strength and integrity of the traditional canon are retained and its works still form the main body of student readings.

Careful attention must be given to add works for the right reasons. The gender, race, or other attributes of authors should be taken into consideration in asking if certain works have been prejudicially excluded, and if they are deserving of a new review. But when such a review is given, it is what a book *says* that should count, not who wrote it. The principles of unity and plurality figure in again here. Works that can add different viewpoints than those that are found in the already existing plurality of the canon deserve consideration for inclusion, and the very best of those works should be selected. But we should have unity in mind as well. While the writings of contemporary dissidents and the works of other cultures may be contrasted with traditional canonical works to highlight political and cultural differences, amidst the differences we may find a common core. We can seek a greater understanding of the human species as a whole, including the possibility of certain universal truths and values. This human unity thesis is at odds with the fundamental thinking of anticanonism, which relies on the argument for pluralism to support the altering of reading lists. But canonists, too, have failed to take proper account of human unity. They have often touted the great books as the basis for human knowledge per se, while at the same time resisting the obvious curricular implication that in trying to understand the human whole it is necessary to cover all angles and consult the widest possible range of books.

The discussion of all of the above points in one book is an ambitious task, to say the least, especially in a fairly brief book. In light of the everpresent risks associated with overview and synthesis, let me make a few explanatory remarks. My historical account is selective but representative: it highlights certain major occurrences and ideas that are most significant in explaining the heritage of the canon and its pedagogy as we know them today in the United States. After beginning in ancient Greece, and taking note of subsequent Pan-European influences, I have placed an emphasis on the English system of schooling out of which our own system developed. Beginning with the eighteenth century, I concentrate solely on our own. I believe this emphasis makes sense, as while there has always been a cross-fertilization between American and European ideas, we have our own distinct model of American education, and many of the Europeans today who come into contact with our canon controversy think it to be quite strange.

Regarding terminology, I have been careful about using the specialized jargon of philosophy and literary theory, at times avoiding it and at other times employing it in ways that can be understood by nonspecialists. It is my hope to reach readers across the spectrum, from scholars engaged directly in the canon controversy, to scholars who are not but are concerned about it, to students affected today by the state of the curriculum, to the educated general public. The term "canon" itself, although not the argot of specialists, also presents a challenge. To avoid the monotony that comes from facing the same word too many times, I have frequently substituted other terms that are used interchangeably. It is interesting to note that while the term "canon" comes to us by way of its ancient and medieval references to standards of truth and sacred texts, it is only in the last couple of decades that the term has resurfaced to refer to student reading lists. Earlier in the twentieth century, the term "great books" was popularized, and there have also been references to "masterpieces" and "masterworks" of the written word. Many earlier educators talked of the "classics," with that term long pointing to the works of Greece and Rome, but later incorporating modern works as well. Few people today would be surprised to hear Shakespeare's works called "classics," and many do not hesitate to apply the word to twentieth century works. I speak of "classics" in both senses and trust the reader to understand the distinction.

Determining the exact boundaries for what the term "canon" or any of its synonyms means is not easy. If fifty different experts were asked to name the contents of the canon, there would be fifty different answers. The various academic fields have their own lists of great works, and we might then think of the canon per se as a combination of those lists that, in order to contract to manageable proportions, takes only the greatest of the great. Still, there has always been much debate over which books have made the final cut. But there is also an element of agreement that has allowed canon supporters to understand one another and work together, and that now allows anticanonists something substantial enough to attack. The canon is sometimes described as being fuzzy around the edges but firm in the middle. That is, it is commonly recognized that works by Plato and Shakespeare belong, but there is considerably less agreement about Epictetus and Balzac. For my purposes, I do not hesitate to name canonical works and authors from the past, or to make suggestions about recent authors who are likely to make the grade. Readers who differ with me over some of the specifics can still follow my line of discussion.

Having said this much about a commonly heard term, I will also say something about an uncommon one. I have chosen "anticanonism" to represent the recent attack on the canon. Among the attackers there are various strains and selected themes that individuals concentrate on. And their prescriptions for what to do about the nemesis canon vary, from angry cries to throw it out, to the more subtle positions that monuments from the past need to be kept on display as a reminder of the evils of the Western cultural tradition, or that the supposedly "great" books should compete for readers' attention with any other vehicles of communication, including graffiti and commercial advertisements. In spite of the different approaches to be found among canon critics, I believe it is possible to present a generic picture, that is, to describe a category. After all, while making different points those critics often work in concert with one another—at academic conferences, in collections of writings, on curriculum committees—against what they see as a common enemy, and their efforts are having a strong collective effect. There is an identifiable anticanon movement—just as there is a recognizable canon—and an explanation of how the various elements of this movement come together should be an asset for anyone trying to make sense of a complex and confusing controversy.

Again, regarding terminology and categorization, I make a distinction between two varieties of canonists: "strict" and "reform." The terms are, of course, borrowed from another context, but I am unaware of their appearing elsewhere concerning the contemporary debate over the great books. The distinction may seem to some readers like an unreal bifurcation, but if they conceive of it as constituting a difference of degree more than of kind, it may be more appealing. Certainly, canonists are not all of the same stripe, and recognizing differences among them is important for understanding the resolution I propose for the great canon controversy.

Finally, let me emphasize two points. One is that the canon I am writing about includes works from various disciplines. While discussion of the canon has sometimes centered on the discipline we call "literature" or the books taught in departments of "English," the canon as a whole is much broader. My approach leaves aside certain matters that are important to the study of literature but are of lesser concern to other disciplines; for instance, the aesthetic dimension and the affective element. I focus on what readers gain from the great books of all disciplines, what canonical works in general have to give, irrespective of their unique disciplinary features.

The other point is that, while I mention many great works and make reference to their basic meanings or messages, I do not engage in close or extended textual analysis. While scholars who are knowledgeable of canonical works might find such an analysis desirable, or to be expected, I will leave that exercise to other authors. My purpose in referring to specific great works is simply to support the overall effort of the book: to survey the main ideas related to the canon controversy, and to synthesize and respond to those ideas with brevity and clarity.

Part I

❧

A BRIEF HISTORY OF
TEACHING THE CANON

THE CANON OF GREAT BOOKS that has been the subject of much controversy in higher education for the past couple of decades had its beginnings in ancient Greece. The list of works that comprise today's canon began forming at that time, and the practice was started of giving those works a central place in schooling. Over the centuries, the list—or lists, if one prefers to think in contemporary terms of the separation of the disciplines—grew to encompass books from the variety of languages and national cultures that we identify as European, or more broadly as Western so as to include American authors and ideas as well. Which canonical works have been in favor with curriculum designers, and how they have been used, has varied over time. But the idea of a canon, agreement about what many of its contents are, and the practice of teaching its works have been present throughout the development of Western culture.

The first canonical works were Homer's *Iliad* and *Odyssey*, which were composed in the eighth century B.C., although they are descriptive of a time several centuries earlier. The poems were disseminated through succeeding generations by rhapsodes (professional reciters), and somewhere along the way were recorded in written form.[1] Homer's works were regarded as masterpieces, and he as having achieved perfection in his art. His accomplishment was at the time the literary equivalent of battlefield heroism or civic leadership. The early Greek system of education was not primarily a literary one, but the portion of it that was focused especially on Homer. Not only had he achieved a type of human perfection, but he described other types through the qualities of his heroes: Nestor's wisdom, Agamemnon's leadership, Ulysses' oratory. Listeners and readers who experienced great epic poetry learned about how great people think and behave. In addition to Homer, the writings of other prominent figures became part of the curriculum. The poetry of Hesiod, and later of Theognis, were popular, as well as the stories of Aesop and the writings of the statesman and lawgiver Solon. A few of the early works are still with us today, and Homer remains a major canonical author. Aesop's name is well known, although the extent to which his stories are actually read could be questioned. Other early authors are relegated to mention only in historical accounts.

By the end of the fifth century B.C., a rich intellectual culture was developing that expanded well beyond poetry to include philosophy, drama, oratory, history, mathematics, and science. Greece was reaching the height of its classical age. Names like Pindar, Sappho, Pythagoras, Herodotus, Aeschylus, and Sophocles had risen to the fore, and were followed in the next several generations by Thucydides, Euripides, Aristophanes, Plato, Aristotle, Demosthenes, and Euclid, all of whom are still recognized today as ancient greats. Informal learning occurred through public performances: historians and philosophers sometimes gave lectures at large, plays were staged in amphitheatres for crowds of many thousands, and rhapsodes still gave recitations of the great poets. Books were readily available. Aristocrats sometimes had personal collections (small by today's standards) that they shared with friends, and in Athens a library open to the public provided copies of popular dramas. Many books could be purchased inexpensively from booksellers, and schoolmasters owned them and children used them in the schools. Later (around 300 B.C.), the Greeks established the famed library of Alexandria, which would stand for several centuries as the greatest collection of books in its time.

Formal schooling grew into the distinct levels of primary, secondary, and higher, with the study of great works being the key to the curriculum, especially at the latter two levels, after basic literacy had been mastered. The program of schooling, however, was not a unitary one. Three different approaches to secondary and higher education grew out of disagreements over the purpose of schooling and what constituted a well-educated person. The ideal of a literate culture was universally respected, and general education, relying heavily on the great books known at the time, figured into all three approaches. The Greeks held a high regard for "polymathy" (literally, a knowledge of all things, although they really meant all intellectual things). But there were differences among them over the reasons for acquiring such broad learning and for knowing the cultural masterpieces.

The Sophists offered a type of schooling that taught public speaking and persuasion; they prepared their students for success in politics and business, where rhetorical competence was of utmost importance. A major portion of the curriculum—and for some of the Sophists, all of it—consisted of learning techniques of speech and engaging in oral argument. Language skills and what today we might call "critical thinking" were the desired outcome. But many of the Sophists offered an expanded program involving other subjects. For developing critical thinking, some included mathematics, because of its tendency for rigorous exercise of the mind in analytics. And considerable importance was placed on a knowledge of great themes or "commonplaces" such as could be found among the great writers of poetry and drama. Students read great works and keyed on standard passages.[2] The rationale was that successful debate, particularly in spontaneous situations, requires "cultural literacy," to again employ present-day lingo; and cultural literacy involves at least a surface acquaintance with the "great ideas." Speakers need to know what they are talking about, or at least sound as if they do. A respected speaker in Greece in the fifth century B.C. was expected to drop names and quote famous expressions, and to discuss issues and put them in perspective.

The Sophists' program was strictly utilitarian, concentrating especially on business and political affairs. While training convincing speakers, they did not aim at developing morality or preparing their students for cultural enjoyments. Their underlying philosophy took a relativist position that denied the existence of absolute right and wrong or true and false, instead emphasizing what their supporters saw as common sense and their detractors as cunning and unprincipled opportunism. They purported that their students would learn to take any side in a debate and make it the winning one. Knowing about great books had a place within the Sophistic approach, but without any designs on truth, goodness, the beauty and enjoyment of learning for its own sake, or other such lofty ideals as supporters of the canon have often prized.

The Platonic system arose in opposition to the Sophists. Plato provided a sketch of his ideal educational plan from the elementary level through the ancient Greek equivalent of graduate school, although as a practicing educator he worked at the level of higher education. Plato opposed the Sophists' relativism, and emphasized that the search for knowledge should be a search for truth and goodness, that is, a search for absolute knowledge, or what philosophers call "universals." Whereas the Sophists wanted to know great ideas for the purpose of using them as rhetorical tools, Plato wanted to explore them in depth, to mine them for right answers about the nature of reality and the most fitting way to live.

Plato proposed having elementary- and secondary-level students read great books, but he was skeptical of their capacity to pick out right from wrong when they encountered the various viewpoints and the many differing depictions of life found in those books. He was critical of Homer and of other authors for portraying sensuousness and highly emotionally charged action. Plato recognized the power of great books as a vehicle for values education; he was an advocate of using them for this purpose, but for the uninitiate he wanted them censored and rewritten so as to present only proper moral standards, only upright thinking and role models. He understood the confusion that can occur in an untrained mind through exposure to a great books reading program, and his answer was to unabashedly tailor the readings to coincide with right thinking.

At the level of higher education, however, Plato emphasized a more open approach that centered on the discussion of great ideas. The aim was to find truth, to know the good, but the method was dialectical. Plato believed that the trained mind could reach toward universals and that the process was facilitated by critical thinking. He wanted to develop the faculty of reason for high-performance functioning, and concurrently point it toward right answers. Mathematics was an important tool for Plato in fostering rigorous use of the mind, but at the highest level of thinking, students applied their mental acuity to key issues in philosophy. They would consider and debate about all proposed or possible positions on topics like what is the nature of courage, of friendship, what is the best form of government, and so on, in hopes of eliminating wrong answers and arriving at the best. Acquaintance with the ideas discussed and the various positions concerning them could be facilitated by reading great books, as well as by prior discussion or suggestions by an instructor. But truth itself would not come from books. Books and other sources of ideas would simply provide material to work with in the dialectical method, the starting point for a long, rigorous, philosophical path.

But that path was seen to have another destination, too. Beyond the moral function of learning, the search for universals provides a special sort of enjoyment. Knowledge can be pursued for its own sake. One can read, or go to the theater, or to an exhibition of art, and imbibe the intellectual stimulation of the experience—do it with no exterior goal in mind (although other ends might derive). Here is the highest level of human activity: intellectualization accompanied by an intrinsic satisfaction. Plato seemed to conceive of this activity as an adult enterprise, as requiring chronological maturity as well as a solid educational foundation. Whether or not he thought secondary-level students were capable of it (although to a lesser extent) is not clear. For them, the reading of great books was at least a preparation for activity for its own sake, even if the ultimate enjoyment was to come only later.

The third approach to secondary and postsecondary schooling in classical Greece, competing with the Sophistic and the Platonic, was the Oratorical. Its most famous proponent was Isocrates, a contemporary of Plato's mentor Socrates. A well-educated person, as we have noted, would have public-speaking skills. The Orators taught grammar and the language of eloquence by having their students read great works of poetry and other subjects. And they wrote their own texts on rhetoric, full of models of persuasion and disputation, which they treated as great works in their own right. Speaking skills, then, were important, but the Orators held such skills to be part and parcel of a greater and more complete human enterprise; facility with words was taken to be the outward manifestation of true human excellence, and an indication of the quality of a person's whole being. Also required was a knowledge of right and wrong. A well-trained orator would be morally upright, and not seek to persuade simply for personal advancement.

The complete human enterprise, however, was recognized to involve even more. Eloquence and morality require an understanding of general culture. In the Oratorical approach, study of the classics—Homer and Hesiod, other poets, the writings of the Sophists and of historians Herodotus and Thucydides, and so on (mathematics was not excluded, but was not held in the high esteem Plato had for it)—was important for learning about one's national culture. The Greeks were proud of their culture and considered it superior to all others, and indeed they exported it to many surrounding peoples. A well-educated person would participate in it, bask in it, and draw from it the necessary elements for successful public speaking and moral living.

The Orators opposed the Sophists' relativism, and held a faith that morality has a solid foundation. They believed that schooling, and especially reading great works, leads to a morally upright person. But they were vague about just how the process of acquiring morality through this means actually occurs. They seemed to assume it would be absorbed or developed, and they focused on the tools for doing so, and on the outcome, without careful attention to the *how* of the occurrence. The Orators also differed from the Sophists regarding the *why* of general education. Both prescribed it and used the great books to teach it. For the Sophists, general education aimed at cultural literacy for use in the art of persuasion, whereas the Orators conceived the passing-on of cultural heritage to be much more. It involved finding the foundation of morality, and development of the whole person into the highest level of human being. Here is the basis for what has come to be referred to as the "humanist" approach to schooling. Culture was considered to be the supreme good, encompassing the elements of oratory and morality, and when viewed in this way, recognized as an end in itself, or perhaps better said, *the* end in itself. As in the case of the Platonic approach, pursuit of something, the end of which is in itself, involves intrinsic satisfaction. Absorbing general culture becomes an enjoyable endeavor operating beyond other endeavors, and justifiable in its completeness over and above them.

But the Orators and Platonists differed over the extent to which, or way in which, receiving cultural heritage relates to the highest level of human activity. The Platonists saw the Orators as assuming them to be identical, as prescribing inert knowledge from the past, as accepting existing doctrines, however "great" they might be, at face value. Isocrates and company were disparaged for not questioning keenly enough and not being critical enough of their great inheritance.[3] In truth, the Orators did not discount new ideas, new books, or other new forms of expression, but they emphasized more than their philosophical rivals did the urge to bask in the glory and greatness that Greek culture had achieved. The debate was about critical thinking versus passive learning, and about accepting one's culture versus questioning it.

The competition among Sophists, Platonists, and Orators acquaints us with many key elements that persist today in the discussion about the value of studying the great books. Few better cases could be made for the contemporary relevance of knowing our historical roots. Studying the canon was found to align with several educational aims. First, the great books were used as an instrument for teaching skills. They offer models of linguistic excellence to be emulated in speaking and writing, and they provide general ideas that can be discussed and debated to hone critical thinking. Second, the great books were employed to immerse their readers in culture. Combined with linguistic and thinking skills, they provide a speaker with cultural literacy, that is, the content needed to be impressive. And beyond cultural literacy, the heritage passed along by the canon can be an enjoyable study in itself, taking the student to an understanding and appreciation that marks the heights of human endeavor. And included in this lofty ideal is the moral fabric of our being. Here is the third main aim of education that the great books were found to serve. They provide models of the sundry ways people have lived their lives, and exhortations about right ways to follow and wrong ways to avoid.

Besides demonstrating the ways the canon is claimed to be used to educational advantage, the Greek experience foreshadows controversy therein. Are the ideas that the canon expresses indicative of a firm epistemological foundation of truth and morality? Or is such a foundation fanciful thinking that should be discarded in favor of a relativist position that denies the existence of universals? Is the canon steeped in objectionable moral content—today's buzzword might be "political"—that students would be better off not being exposed to, or that they will have to be disabused of? And, if the great ideas expressed in the great books are accepted as appropriate subject matter, to what extent should students absorb and revere them, and to what extent should they dissect, argue with, and perhaps revise or reject them? In other words, is the canon a repository of treasures, or the stuff for critical minds to approach with a deconstructive bent?

As the classical age of Greece passed into the Hellenistic age, the educational approach of the Orators won out over its rivals. The Sophists were a phenomenon of the fifth century B.C., although their influence was not forgotten. The Platonic approach maintained a sector of higher education, and was to a degree borrowed by the more philosophically minded Orators. But the Oratorical model prevailed as the one to which most students were exposed. Emphasis was not so much on developing students' reasoning capacity as on passing along the growing heritage of masterpieces. Canonization was a main focus among the keepers of culture, especially those who arranged the curriculum. Lists became popular, often numbered: ten historians, seven plays by Sophocles, and so on. In fact, the only plays existing today from Sophocles, Aeschylus, and Aristophanes are ones selected by editors for teaching purposes.

By the second or first century B.C., the secondary-school curriculum was based especially on four authors: Homer for epic poetry, Euripides for tragic drama, Menander for comedic drama, and Demosthenes for oratory. They were complemented by various other names, including not only the earlier-mentioned greats whom we still recognize today, but others who are now relegated to footnotes and largely forgotten even by specialists.[4]

Mathematics and science, or collectively, the mathematical sciences, were sometimes divided into arithmetic, geometry, astronomy, and music (harmonics). That four-part schema, eventually to become the medieval *quadrivium*, traces back to Pythagoras in the sixth century B.C. But the emphasis in Hellenistic education was on the humanities, what would become the *trivium* of grammar, rhetoric, and logic, and was to be found especially in works of literature and history, along with oratory and philosophy.

The latter subject was reserved for higher education, as it had been in Plato's time. And at that level, schools of philosophy competed with schools of rhetoric as the two types of formal higher schooling available. The curriculum of the latter followed upon that of rhetoric at the secondary level. It consisted in part of studying the great works of oratory and history, with the tradition of each school built especially around a particular figure such as Demosthenes, Lysias, and so on. But a good deal of the program involved practice at oral exercises, in which students declaimed on topics assigned by the instructors. The philosophical schools also followed particular traditions: Platonism, Aristotelianism, Stoicism, Epicureanism, Skepticism. Generally, they taught something of the history of philosophy (pre-Socratics: Thales, Pythagoras, Democritus, and so on) and of their contemporary rival schools, but each concentrated mainly on its own classics, including those of the respective founders: Plato, Aristotle, Zeno, Epicurus, Pyrrho, and other leading figures. The great works of Greek philosophy, while not read in secondary schools, became preserved for posterity at the collegiate level, although only a small portion of the population actually studied them.

Taking form parallel to Greek Hellenistic schooling, and borrowing from it, was Roman schooling. As the Roman Empire expanded and annexed large territories, much of it included Greek-speaking peoples. The Romans quickly recognized the subtleties with language usage and analysis that Greek rhetors had achieved, and the great books the Greek heritage was passing on. The Greeks' national pride, as well as the fact that they were the inventors of certain forms of discourse and kinds of learning, led them to limit their objects of reverence and the curriculum in their schools largely, if not exclusively, to things Greek. They had communication and commerce with other peoples, but the culture they valued was their own. The Romans, on the other hand, were willing to assimilate and continue foreign intellectual accomplishments they found of value. They had their own Latin language and developing culture in which they eventually could take pride. But learning to speak, read, and write Greek became important for status-conscious Romans and for those who truly wanted the highest form of available culture, including successful public speaking. Roman education imported Greeks at first to teach the language and its classics, with Romans eventually acquiring the expertise and assuming the responsibility.

Latin, of course, was also studied, with the educational system developing along bilingual lines. Students learned both languages, and the program of secondary education was based on readings from the Hellenistic canon as well as newly written Latin works that achieved immediate and eventually equal status. By the time of the late Empire, the four featured Latin authors were Virgil, Terence, Sallust, and Cicero. Other prominent authors included Horace, Ennius, Ovid, Lucan, Nero, and Statius.

Mathematics and science were, in theory, part of the curriculum, although in reality they were given little attention. Prominent educational theorists such as Quintilian and Cicero issued paeans to their worth, but study of those subjects, and reading from their great works, was reserved for a few people with special talents for them.

The ideal of secondary education was the Greek Oratorical one. The aim was to produce a skilled speaker and morally upright person who was acquainted with general culture through a broad array of great literature. The Romans continued the Greeks' respect for polymathy; it is summed up well in Cicero's formula for what makes a great orator:

In my opinion, indeed, no man can be an orator possessed of every praiseworthy accomplishment, unless he has attained the knowledge of everything important, and of all liberal arts, for his language must be ornate and copious from knowledge, since, unless there be beneath the surface matter understood and felt by the speaker, oratory becomes an empty and puerile flow of words.[5]

Cicero here speaks of what were coming to be called the "liberal arts." Together they constituted a comprehensive general education, which eventually became rigidified into the seven divisions of the *trivium* and *quadrivium*. Knowledge of the liberal arts, gained especially through an acquaintance with great books, characterized the cultured person and was the province of secondary schooling. Higher education for the Romans comprised specialized training. Greek schools of philosophy continued to exist well into the time of Roman occupation, and were one alternative for postsecondary possibilities. But the Romans preferred advanced study in their own schools of rhetoric (the main form of higher schooling), or in their own unique contribution to the history of education—the formal study of law. The former concentrated on oral exercises in speechmaking, conducted in much the same way as the Greeks did. Aside from the classics of oratory, attention to the great books seems to have been assumed, and left to the secondary schools. The teaching of law established its own canon of readings by Hadrian and others. Here again the approach of studying masterworks and great ideas was followed, but limited to the specialized field of study.

Outside of formal schooling, the Romans made books an important cultural interest. It was routine for a patrician household to have its own library, and many were large and lavishly furnished. In the city of Rome a system of public libraries was established, including a large research collection. Through conquest the Romans acquired Greek collections, among which was the library of Pergamum (perhaps two hundred thousand volumes), reportedly given as a gift by Antony to Cleopatra and moved to Alexandria. Roman booksellers sold books cheaply, and an entire street of the city was devoted to that trade. Outside the city, books were exported throughout the Empire.

As the Roman Empire continued for several centuries, and passed into its decline on the way to early medieval times, several circumstances appeared that shrunk the orbit of secondary and higher education, lessened the availability of books, and reduced study of the great books to a mere shadow of the practice begun in Greece. Gradually, the Greek language and its literature were eclipsed by Latin and its growing list of great works. Cicero's writings were particularly significant in this regard, as they demonstrated that the Latin language was capable of eloquence and sophisticated rhetoric rivaling that of Greek. Roman culture had come of age, and was asserting itself. The newly established Christian church, soon to become the dominant force in the Western world for many centuries, also contributed to the demise of Greek, as it began using Latin in its services and writings. Gradually, some of the Greek classics were translated into Latin, teachers of Greek became scarce, and the language faded away in the schools. Such was the fate of Greek in the Western Empire, although in the Eastern Empire it remained alive. But the Eastern Empire was shut off from the West by the great division that existed between Constantinople and Rome. That division was notably along religious lines, but it was linguistic and cultural as well. The East preserved the Greek language and its classics throughout the darkest of medieval times, while Western Europe went without. The revival of the Greek classics in the West, beginning in the twelfth century, would rely heavily upon the efforts of scholars from the East, most significantly on Arab scholars, whose contact with the Greek language led them to an appreciation of Greek philosophy. Before that revival is described, however, other factors should be taken into account that contributed to the decline of the ancient canon, not only its Greek portion, but the Latin portion as well.

As the Empire fell, much of literate culture was lost or submerged. Libraries were destroyed during warfare as various invaders overran the Roman world, including the library at Alexandria, said to contain from half a million to a million volumes.[6] Numerous great works vanished from existence in this way. Historical references tell us, for instance, of many philosophical works (dialogues by Aristotle, and the writings of the pre-Socratics) and plays (by Aeschylus, Sophocles, and others) that were lost. Much of the process of deciding which authors and works from the ancient world would eventually be selected for inclusion in the modern canon occurred through decimation and default.

Literacy declined as schools disappeared. The preservation of reading and of books became the province of the church. But since its inception, the church had not been a major force in providing general schooling. Early Christians sent their children to Roman schools for basic learning, with church-sponsored learning limited to religious teachings. With the demise of secular schools, eventually the only centers of literacy were the monasteries, where training was reserved for the clergy and their novices.

The program of study in the monasteries was oriented toward religion. The aim of education underwent a shift in which the ideals of intellectualization for its own sake and schooling to prepare for civic life and leadership were replaced by devotion to God. Moral education was still of concern, but within the orbit of religion. The principal book to be read was the Bible, the Latin or Vulgate version of which was prepared by Saint Jerome in the latter fourth century. It included the Old Testament or Hebrew Bible, written beginning at approximately the time of Homer, as well as the New Testament, which appeared during later Roman times with the advent of Christianity. But with the Bible established as the authoritative written word, and supported by other Christian documents, a strong tension was felt between these writings and the pagan writings of the Greeks and Romans. The problem of pagan literature, sensed by early Christians but tolerated in their religion's infancy, soon became a major concern that was to last for several centuries.

The educational tradition the monasteries inherited was based on the classics. Through these books students learned the church's official language of Latin, and also many of the categories of thought (especially from Greek philosophy) an educated person and mature thinker needed to be acquainted with. But the classics also contain stories of non-Christian gods and orgiastic rituals, and ideas about the nature of the universe and humanity that conflicted with church teachings. Religious leaders feared that a general education in pagan literature as the basis for higher studies in the Christian religion endangered students by encouraging in them thoughts and emotions that were difficult to overcome. The great books were seen as temptresses, as singing a siren song to which impressionable readers would succumb. Church councils discussed the problem, and various decrees were issued condemning non-Christian writings and emphasizing the superiority of the Bible. The *Didascalia Apostolorum*, a third-century document, exemplified the gravity of the matter. "Have nothing to do with heathen writings," it directed, "and refrain from strange discourses, laws, or false prophets. . . . If you will explore history, you will have the Book of Kings; or if you seek words of wisdom and eloquence you have the Prophets, Job, and the Book of Proverbs, wherein you will find a more perfect knowledge. . . ."[7]

But old habits did not die easily. Major figures like Jerome, Augustine, and Pope Gregory condemned pagan books, yet with stirring confessions of regret returned to them time and again in their own readings, and continued to refer to them in the works they wrote. While afraid of the destructive potential of the classics, they realized, too, their value, and could not give up such cultural treasures. Apologies for the continuance of pagan works employed curious metaphors, both Biblical and earthy. One explanation refers to Deuteronomy where an Israelite might take a captive maid: "Whatsoever is in her of love, of wantonness, of idolatry, I shave; and having made of her an Israelite indeed, I beget sons unto the Lord." Another explanation notes Apollo and the Muses, and Orpheus and Eurydice, and says, "The King of Heaven sets his curse upon suchlike leasings. Why then do I harp upon them? . . . Since even as dung spread upon the field enriches it to good harvest, so the filthy writings of the pagan poets are a mighty aid to divine eloquence."[8]

"Shaving," to make use of that metaphor, often consisted of editing out offensive passages and presenting students with the remainder. Another strategy, making use of "dung" to generate "divine eloquence," was to focus on the *form* of classical writings (the grammar and rhetoric) while issuing watchful reminders to students about unacceptable *content*. A third approach interpreted the great pagan works as pre-Christian configurations of the divine word. The Bible, in this view, held the final answers; the Greek and Roman classics were eloquent but sometimes confused or mistaken attempts to work out those answers.

The upshot of the church's ambivalent affair with pagan literature was that during the lowest point in the history of Western education and culture (the sixth, seventh, and eighth centuries), a respect for the classics was carried on, but contact with the books themselves occurred guardedly and sparingly. The curriculum students followed in preparation for theological studies involved selected ideas from the ancient learning, as it was classified under the seven liberal arts (with emphasis on grammar and rhetoric). But exposure to the classics was minimal compared with previous and subsequent ages, and was often indirect. While there was some reading from primary sources, the most common presentation was through texts and encyclopedic works that provided summaries and quotations. Such books, some of the most widely used of which were prepared by Donatus, Cassiodorus, Isidore, Priscian, Martianus Capella, and Bede, are today considered to be inferior relics, even by devout keepers of the canon. The names of their authors have long since lapsed into obscurity.

Later Roman and early medieval times were not a period for the production of great writings, although along with the New Testament, a few other works did appear that show through in the canon today. The *Confessions* and *City of God* by Augustine are examples, as is *The Consolation of Philosophy* by Boethius. It is important to remember the dominant position of Latin as the language of the learned. Modern languages were in their early development, and they generated a good deal of oral composition of poetry, as well as some written. Occasionally, examples of these early poems are included today in anthologies of national literatures, but with the exceptions of *Beowulf* (eighth century) in English (actually Old English, a form quite foreign to Modern English users, and needing entire translation) and *The Song of Roland* (we leap to the eleventh century for the first significant work in French), we wait until the Renaissance for literature in native tongues that would go on to achieve canonical status. And even then, it would be several centuries more before vernacular works would overcome the stigma of being second-rate to Latin, and begin to work their way into the curriculum of the schools.

Near the beginning of the ninth century, study of the great books experienced a moderate revival inspired by the influence of Charlemagne. He made unusual efforts to establish a widespread system of schools that would raise the educational level of the clergy, the nobility, and also the common people. And he himself attempted (although with little success) to become literate not only in Latin but also in Greek. His chief educational minister, Alcuin, promoted the study of classical learning, although he had essentially the same limited list of books to work from as had been in use for several centuries. The curriculum over which he presided was state of the art for the early medieval period. For grammar, students read texts by Priscian and Donatus; for rhetoric, Cicero and Quintilian; and for logic, Porphyry and Aristotle (the *Categories* and *On Interpretation*, two of Aristotle's minor works, but the only ones of his available during the Middle Ages). Arithmetic was learned from Bede, geometry from a summary of some elementary points from Euclid. The books for astronomy were by Pliny and Bede, and for music, books by Bede and Boethius. General summaries (encyclopedias) added to these books included those of Isidore, Bede, and Alcuin.[9] Not all of these subjects or works were given equal attention, however: the *trivium* was emphasized over the *quadrivium*, and of the *trivium*, logic was less emphasized than grammar and rhetoric. The Oratorical model still held sway.

Other books were, of course, available for ambitious students and for scholars who were advanced beyond the basic curriculum. Alcuin spoke of the library at York, mentioning some forty works in particular: numerous Church fathers, several of the Latin classics, some grammarians, and some late Christian writers.[10] The size of a monastery library at this time might have run to a few hundred volumes, as collections often were smaller than the personal libraries found in the homes of intellectuals today. In response to the limited availability of books, Alcuin instituted an extensive program for copying Latin manuscripts, including many of the classics.

The "Carolingian renaissance," as Charlemagne's time has sometimes been called, brightened the prospects for renewed interest in classical learning. But the true rebirth came in two further phases, the second of which also contributed numerous great books to the canon that students are exposed to today. The Renaissance of the fourteenth through sixteenth centuries was preceded by a recovery of the Greek philosophical and scientific classics and a period of intense philosophical and theological activity.

When the Greek language was lost in Europe, it survived in the Byzantine world. There, beginning in the eighth century, Arab scholars translated many Greek works into their own language. Among the more noted translators were Avicenna, Averroes, and Omar Khayyam, whose poem *The Rubaiyat* later became immortalized in English literature. With the advent of the Muslim religion and its rapid spread to control much of the Mediterranean area, Spain became one of its major cultural centers. During the twelfth and thirteenth centuries, Latin scholars traveled to Spain, learned Arabic, sought out Arabic editions of important Greek works, and translated them into Latin. Other translating activity was centered in Sicily, another Muslim stronghold, and in pockets of northern Italy. There, manuscripts in the original Greek were available (some brought from the East, and some probably preserved there throughout the middle ages), and as Western scholars familiarized themselves with the language, they transferred their findings into Latin.

The initial recovery of lost Greek treasures centered on philosophy and science. These are the fields pursued by the Arab scholars who made the recovery possible. They had little interest in Greek drama, poetry, or history, but they marveled at Greek philosophy. Further, their own scientific accomplishments surpassed anything Europe had to offer. Latin scholars eagerly pursued the philosophy and science made available to them, and by the end of the thirteenth century possessed all of Aristotle's works, Greek and Arab medicine and mathematics (including the adoption of Arabic numbers), and works from India, Syria, and Persia.

While Europe was reacquiring these intellectual riches from the East, it was experiencing the birth of its modern system of higher education. Earlier medieval monastic schools eventually spawned counterpart cathedral schools, some of which grew into the first universities: Bologna, Paris, and Oxford among those in the twelfth century, and about seventy-five throughout Europe by the beginning of the sixteenth century.[11] Latin continued to be the universal language of instruction, and the curriculum varied little from school to school. "Majors" were available in medicine, law, and theology, but the arts program provided an extensive general education. It continued to follow the *trivium* and *quadrivium* of the prior centuries, and some of the same texts. But now there was notable enrichment. The arts program at Oxford in the mid-thirteenth century reflected the strong influence of the recovered works of Aristotle. It began with grammar from Priscian and Donatus, followed by logic from Boethius and Aristotle (now not limited to the two books studied in the earlier Middle Ages, but including the meat of Aristotle's treatment of the subject—the *Prior Analytics* and *Posterior Analytics*), and rhetoric from Aristotle, Cicero, and Boethius. It continued with arithmetic and music from Boethius, geometry from Euclid (a more thorough treatment than was given earlier), astronomy from Ptolemy, and Aristotle's natural, moral, and mental philosophies. Medical students studied Galen and Hippocrates, Isaac on fevers, and Nicholas on pharmacology. The theology course centered on the Bible and the *Sentences* of Peter Lombard, and the courses on law studied Justinian's civil law, Gratian's synthesis of church law, and the decrees of Gregory IX and his successors.[12]

The church was still the dominant force in society during this period, and intellectual culture was saturated by theological concerns. It was the age of "scholasticism," during which the study of philosophy intermingled with theology to produce many subtle analyses of the nature of God, and how and to what extent human beings can come to know their creator. Authors such as Anselm, Bonaventure, Duns Scotus, and Ockham wrote works that were much discussed at the time, but that today are likely to be skipped over in philosophy and religion courses, with Thomas Aquinas's *Summa Theologica* often listed as the sole representative book of later medieval thinking.

Scholasticism diminished the importance of grammar and rhetoric, and advanced the cause of logic, additional areas of philosophy, and, to some extent, the *quadrivium*. The ideally educated person was now inspired more by philosophy than by the Oratorical ideal.

Still, that ideal remained present, if temporarily less powerful. The renewed interest in Greek philosophy signaled that there was now little fear of reading pagan classics, and those scholars who had a bent toward Roman literature were more free to pursue it. Someone well read in this area would know Virgil, Horace, Ovid, Sallust, Cicero (more than the basics), Petronius, Seneca, Quintilian, Plautus, Terence, and others.[13] The time was ripe for the rediscovery of their Greek counterparts.

The translation efforts on Greek manuscripts that began in Italy with scientific and philosophical works in the twelfth century continued in the fourteenth century with a shift to poetry, drama, and history. These were among the chief interests of the Renaissance "humanists," who avidly pursued the ancient writings of the Romans and those now newly available of the Greeks in Latin translation. And while the early humanists read the Greek works in this way, later generations gained a knowledge of the language and read those works in the original. Homer and company regained a place among the great books to which a well-educated person would be exposed, and the Greek language was revived and made a desired intellectual accomplishment. Outside of Italy this process began in the fifteenth century, and with the invention of movable type early in the century, by its close the classics of Greek and Roman authors were being produced by this means.

Humanism opposed and even ridiculed scholasticism as overly pedantic specialization that narrowed the natural field of intellectual inquiry and failed to speak to the everyday concerns of most human beings. A new outlook about life and learning emerged, as religion was not cast out, but reduced from its position of overt dominance. Worldly concerns, as opposed to other-worldly ones, captured humanist interest, although many of the authors were themselves devout churchmen. An outpouring of writings that announced the new outlook included many that later became part of the canon we know today. Dante's *Divine Comedy* is sometimes listed as the first here, although it was more an expression of medieval ideals than those of the Renaissance. Dante was followed by Petrarch, who left many sonnets, and devoted much of his life to copying and editing classical manuscripts. Other works include

Pico's *On the Dignity of Man*, Machiavelli's *The Prince*, Boccaccio's *Decameron*, Cervantes' *Don Quixote*, Chaucer's *Canterbury Tales*, Spenser's *Faerie Queene*, Erasmus's *In Praise of Folly*, Rabelais's *Gargantua and Pantagruel*, and More's *Utopia*. And, as the Renaissance moved forward into the Reformation, the writings of Luther and Calvin especially, among the Protestant reformers, continued the humanist ideals.

Humanism's effect on education appeared at the secondary level before reaching the universities. Eventually, it captured much of higher education as well, although scholastic-type institutions continued to exist. The effect on the curriculum was to expand study of the ancient great books to the point where the list comprised most of what students read. The Greek and Roman masterpieces were now approached not simply as necessary or helpful tools for developing facility with language and ideas as a basis for further studies. The ancient Oratorical ideal came back in full force, as the goals of education again became moral, civic, and cultural. Students were to grow to an understanding of life through great works, prepare for nonclerical careers, and experience learning and books as enjoyable pursuits for their own sake. All of these aims were enmeshed with an aristocratic perspective of education for an elite, which grew into the gentlemanly ideal of classical learning as befitting a man of high social standing and making him worthy of his separation from the masses. The authors that were read to accomplish these goals included the list of Romans that under scholasticism would have been left to specialist scholars in belles lettres. Now they became standard fare for undergraduate students. And to the Romans were added the Greeks: Homer and the poets, the playwrights, Thucydides, Xenophon, Plutarch, Demosthenes, Isocrates, and so on. Although not absent from the program, philosophy was not emphasized, and the Roman classics and language got more attention than the Greek.

In an interesting paradox regarding language, Renaissance secondary schools sometimes taught the vernacular, and some of the humanists supported that practice. And many of the great humanist writings were written in the vernacular. Yet humanism still emphasized a reverence for classical learning, and supported the teaching of the classical languages as the essence of a superior education. Preparation for the mundane affairs of life was facilitated by learning the languages in which those affairs were conducted, but a solid secondary education, and certainly higher education, involved facility with the classical languages and reading the masterpieces written in them. Even such a biting critic of the "old" (scholastic) education as Rabelais has his famous character, Gargantua, recommend to his son Pantagruel to learn "first the Greek as Quintilian advises; secondly the Latin; and finally the Hebrew, for sake of the Holy Scriptures, along with the Chaldaic and the Arabic, for the same purpose."[14] The humanists held facility with languages in esteem, and in fact, ventured beyond the bounds of Latin and Greek. But when they did so, they demonstrated a leaning toward the ancient world. Humanism was influential in introducing the vernacular into the schools, but also played a role in limiting its influence. While the new curriculum expanded languages and reading materials considerably, the most respected language-learning looked backward in time more than to the present or future for its inspiration.

The humanist curriculum continued to hold sway through the seventeenth century. Secondary schools concentrated on teaching the Latin and Greek languages and some of their great works (a bit of Hebrew was taught by some schools as a prestigious "ornament"); universities focused on a longer list of those works, and they were read more thoroughly. Programs began to vary more from one university to another, and in England there were differences between the recommended reading list of one tutor and that of another, as the tutorial system became firmly established there. But the variance generally consisted of decisions about which Greek and Roman authors to include and which not to. A medieval work might be included on occasion, or perhaps a Renaissance work like Erasmus's *Colloquies*, but for the most part the curriculum resisted change as the Renaissance gave way to the Enlightenment. Intellectual culture then underwent another metamorphosis that occurred largely outside of educational institutions, but offered them a profound challenge.

The generic concept behind the new Enlightenment thinking was progress, the idea that newer is better. The previous cultural transformation by humanism looked backward for its inspiration;

the new outlook gazed toward the future. There was a confidence that new knowledge was in the making, that truths were forthcoming that had previously eluded even the best minds, especially those of the venerated ancients. In science there were new discoveries and applications by Copernicus (a sixteenth-century figure whose ideas were spreading), Kepler, Galileo, Harvey, Huygens, and Newton. They challenged conventional beliefs in astronomy, added to knowledge about human physiology, and developed the calculus. In doing so they created whole new systems or frameworks for thinking about their fields, a trait they shared with the great philosophers of modernity: Bacon and Hobbes, the "rationalists" Descartes, Spinoza, and Leibnitz, and the "empiricists" Locke, Berkeley, and Hume. Modern philosophy often sounded scientific (or mathematical) as it turned away from previous thinking and offered entire replacements for older systems of metaphysics, epistemology, and ethics. And not to be forgotten were the new perspectives in politics offered by some of the same philosophers as well as Rousseau, and in economics by Adam Smith.

The new thinking also extended to languages. More and more vernacular works of quality were being written as authors increasingly turned toward modern languages as their means of expression. The employment of those languages in scholarly pursuits was touted as a worthy alternative to Latin. As the French encyclopedist d'Alembert put it, "men of letters turned their thoughts to perfecting the vulgar tongues . . . no longer limited themselves to copying the Romans and Greeks, or even to imitating them; they tried to surpass them."[15] D'Alembert was confident that progress was afoot in all areas of intellectual inquiry. The use of the vernacular was a symbol or indication of the great ideas that were contained in many new works, not only in science and philosophy, but in literature as well. During the seventeenth and eighteenth centuries, the likes of Shakespeare, Moliere, Milton, Pope, Racine, Swift, Defoe, Fielding, and Voltaire produced masterpieces still with us today. Of special note was the development of the novel as a modern form of literary presentation.

However, not all Enlightenment thinkers were as enthusiastic as d'Alembert about progress occurring in all fields. They introduced a distinction, still with us today, between the humanities and sciences by which the sciences are characterized as progressive and the humanities not. In earlier times the *trivium*, as opposed to the *quadrivium*, had provided a basis for separating these areas of knowledge, but now the distinction was redefined. In the sciences, it was said, knowledge is cumulative and eliminative, that is, over time new ideas come along that absorb or supersede older ones that are then discarded. Clearly newer is better, as seen in the replacement of Ptolemy's astronomy by that of Copernicus. Compared to science, literature is noncumulative. As new works appear, even if they are in modern languages and perhaps in such a modern form as the novel, the messages they convey do not replace those of their predecessors. Homer's portrayal of Achilles' anger, and Sophocles' of Antigone's defiance of the law, describe thoughts and emotions that have not been superseded through the centuries, but that modern authors, too, may depict, although in different settings.

This distinction has the weakness of not being able to categorize the works of all fields as neatly as, say, astronomy and literature. Philosophy sometimes seems like science, but at other times it is more akin to literature. And the same holds for the social sciences. But the distinction has influenced the way educators have divided up the curriculum, and in particular how they have approached the use of classic works. To proponents of progress, cumulative knowledge is superior since it improves over time. This way of thinking invites us to treat classic works as historical relics or to abandon them altogether in favor of newer improved ones, and it tends to depreciate the value of the humanities. However, there is another perspective on the cumulative/noncumulative distinction that reverses the priorities. The unchanging nature of noncumulative knowledge is seen as its strength. While science changes, even if for the better, it is thus unstable and unfinished. The humanities get at the true and solid foundation of things, and do so through classics that remain alive and contemporary through the passage of time.

These opposing perspectives on cumulative versus noncumulative knowledge describe the basic lines of thought that provoked a major intellectual controversy in England and France during the seventeenth and eighteenth centuries that came to be known as the "quarrel between ancients and moderns," or the "battle of the books." While some Enlightment thinkers championed the cause of progress through new knowledge, a strong counteractive force was marshaled by traditionalists. The idea that post-Renaissance culture was surpassing all that preceded it was seen as unwarranted hubris. A strong caution was urged that moderns should respect the limitations of human nature just as the ancients had done, rather than rush into attempts at perfection. Jonathan Swift spoke for the traditionalist position in his famous fable of the spider and the bee, a preliminary bout in his satirical account of the battle of the books in the Saint James Library. He lampooned modernism in the guise of the spider: "was ever anything so modern as the spider in air, his turns, and his paradoxes? . . . he spins and spits wholly from himself" and "produces nothing at last but flybane and a cobweb."[16] A cobweb is intricate and beautiful, but flimsy and short-lived; it has little substance. The new knowledge, as the traditionalists saw it, was dazzling, dizzying, but without really revealing the nature of things and without providing usable answers that have firm groundings. It appeared as pretty system-building that was subject to whim and vicissitude. So, rather than providing truths that had eluded the ancients, it simply offered change in the form of creative confusion.

What the ancients, on the other hand, had to offer, was represented by the bee, who labors with the materials nature provides and "by an universal range, with long search, much study, true judgment, and distinction of things, brings home honey and wax."[17] In other words, while modernism was overeager to theorize, the ancients and their later followers were content to observe the world, experience it as given, and live their lives based on the information obtained in this way. The ancients stand for the solidity and practicality of a longstanding tradition.

A fair account of the battle of the books holds that it ended in a draw, each side gaining in its own way. Traditionalist supporters of the ancients retained control of the curriculum in the schools, and they would do so until the nineteenth century. But they had been put on notice that modernism's force was not to be taken lightly, and that they were now in a defensive posture that could eventually require a stronger bulwark than was evident so far. What the modernists had gained at this point was considerable, in the larger culture beyond formal schooling. Modern science drew respect, especially in its separation from the humanities. The new brands of philosophy and new ventures in belles lettres were not only popular, but by the end of the eighteenth century had demonstrated staying power. While the ancient classics of the humanities were what was studied in the schools, a well-read person would know the moderns as well, including those beyond the humanities.

While Europe debated the value of ancients versus moderns, the American colonies were established and the American system of schooling began to develop. Elementary schools taught the three R's, and secondary "grammar" schools (for the small portion of the population who reached this level) were devoted to the ancient languages and literature in preparation for college. By the time of the American Revolution, a dozen colleges were in existence, most of them what eventually became the Ivy League universities. They offered largely the same program of study to all students, with little variance from one institution to another, and a single degree without majors or specializations. They served the undergraduate function of providing a general education to an elite group of men who then, through further study (self-directed, apprenticeship, or by traveling to Europe to study at a university there), would enter the professions and take on leadership roles in their society. The curriculum, following the tradition of the European undergraduate arts program of the day, was steeped in ancient authors, along with the study of mathematics and a bit of science. Also included were declamation and disputation in English, to develop oratorical skill in the language of general discourse. Works of modern poets, novelists, and essayists were seldom read in this connection; the practice of reading literature was allied with the ancient languages, and modern authors were not yet rated as academic equivalents to their forebears.

As in Europe, the impact of the Enlightenment in the colonies occurred first outside of formal schooling. Much of the intellectual life was carried on informally, and eventually through organized efforts like the American Philosophical Society. The first strong evidence of the new thinking in the schools came with the academy movement beginning in the mid-eighteenth century. The hardships of living in a physically raw environment instilled in American minds a bent toward practicality that led many to embrace this new type of institution (actually, borrowed from nontraditionalist educators in England). The academy was meant as an alternative form of secondary schooling, and to some extent as a substitute for college as well, although graduates sometimes went on to pursue college studies.

In the spirit of practicality, academies emphasized the English language, and taught applied sciences such as geography, mechanics, and agriculture. They also sometimes taught modern European languages. Their aim was to prepare students for an everyday world in which they needed to communicate in the vernacular and make a living. But even these most "progressive" schools of their time showed respect for traditional humanistic learning, and devoted a significant part of the curriculum to it. Benjamin Franklin, leader of the academy movement in the colonies, and a critic of humanistic overemphasis on ancient learning, still said that youths should be told that "the finest Writings, the most correct Compositions, the most perfect Productions of human Wit and Wisdom" are in Latin and Greek.[18] He recommended study of the classical languages as a distinguishing ornament, but more importantly as a practical necessity for students preparing for careers in the ministry, medicine, or law. And he suggested that all students read from the classics in translation in order to secure a proper foundation in history and morals. Thus humanistic learning was still recognized as proper for an elite, although the academists conceived of that elite in professional more than social terms, and a vestige of the model still shone through for other students as well.

As academies grew in numbers and influence during the latter eighteenth and early nineteenth centuries, colleges, too, eventually evidenced the impact of the new learning. The first movement in that direction was toward modern science and philosophy (including or allied with theology). The College of Philadelphia, founded in 1756 (later to become the University of Pennsylvania), was an early leader in introducing modern authors into the curriculum. Representative ancient poets, philosophers, historians, and orators accounted for a good portion of the readings, but a greater number of moderns more than balanced the scale. Bacon, Newton, Locke, Hutcheson, Dryden, and Montesquieu highlighted a long list of names, many of which are little known today.[19] Science occupied a fair share of the curriculum, and the recentness of the works selected in that area, compared with an emphasis on ancients in belles lettres, reflected the distinction between science and the humanities as cumulative/noncumulative.

While the College of Philadelphia opened its curriculum sooner and wider to modern science and philosophy than other institutions did, it is notable that modern languages and literature were still largely absent. The dominance of the ancients in these areas continued, but with ever-increasing tension. There was much debate about the reputed superiority of Greek and Latin studies, with Yale University in 1828 issuing a prominent report that defended the ancients as best. The ideal of the educated gentleman was in the background, the elite man possessing a general knowledge of many fields of study, a man of taste and breeding, a morally upright man. The classics were still assumed to be instrumental in educating such a person, but now the thrust of the argument for them relied not only on claiming their superior cultural content, but on emphasizing that they engage readers' mental processes in a uniquely rigorous and comprehensive fashion. The Yale report describes the most important learning college students can gain as "discipline and furniture of the mind," or in today's terminology, thinking skills and great ideas. The mind, this argument goes, experiences multiform expansion by studying ancient languages and literature:

> The range of classical study extends from the elements of language, to the most difficult questions arising from literary research and criticism. Every faculty of the mind is employed; not only the memory, judgment, and reasoning powers, but the taste and fancey are occupied and improved.[20]

The classics were held to sharpen students' thinking in a way superior to modern works. The latter were rated as social accomplishments and feminine studies; traditionalist scholars held them to be interesting, perhaps even provocative, but intellectually light-weight.

Argumentation such as this allowed the study of ancient litera-ture to hold sway over modern for two or three more decades. The curriculum at most colleges was roughly equivalent to what the College of Philadelphia had introduced a century earlier, with the addition of such later works as William Paley on natural theology, Thomas Reid on mental philosophy, Charles Lyell on geology, and *The Federalist Papers*. Still in effect was the practice that all students at a college followed its uniform course of study; there were not yet separate majors or programs.

From midcentury to its end, curriculum change took hold and moved quickly. The modern high school evolved, growing out of a convergence of the academy and the traditional "grammar" school. The curriculum varied considerably among high schools, but in general, the teaching of Greek and Latin diminished and more emphasis was placed on English and modern foreign languages. Still, the ancient languages were respected, and at least Latin was consid-ered important for those students who were considering college.

Colleges during this period began to embrace English-language literature. At first, students with this interest pursued it through extracurricular literary societies, and by listening to college-sponsored speakers who were important figures in contemporary letters: Emerson, Whitman, and Matthew Arnold. The popularity of English-language letters among students added pressure for their incorporation into the regular curriculum. The movement toward this final mark of respectability began around the time of the Civil War, with Lafayette College as an initiator in 1855. In 1865, Har-vard began a requirement in reading English, and in a few years it grew into a written critique of Shakespeare's plays and Scott's *Ivanhoe*.[21] Other colleges quickly followed suit.

Accompanying the acceptance of English letters were the study of other modern languages and the reading of literature written in those languages. These pursuits, too, had been treated previously as extracurricular, but now gained credit-bearing status. Novels, plays, poetry, and essays were read sometimes in the original language, but often in English translation. With several earlier centuries' worth of great modern literary works now eligible to be considered for inclusion in the humanities portion of the curriculum, some of them inevitably replaced some of the ancients. Further, the nineteenth century was adding many new works of its own. With philosophy already in the practice of balancing ancients with moderns, and literature now starting to do so, figures like Hegel, Goethe, Austen, Schopenhauer, Dickens, Kierkegaard, Eliot, Melville, Dostoevsky, Flaubert, Ibsen, Tolstoy, Twain, James, and Nietzsche demanded attention.

And amidst this flurry of activity, the social sciences arose as a new field of study. They developed at first out of political philosophy, as it had grown the branches of economics and sociology. The works of Smith, Bentham, Mill, Marx, Tocqueville, and others from the latter eighteenth and early to mid-nineteenth centuries provided the groundwork. In the latter part of the century there was a more conscious and rigorous effort to follow the methodology borrowed from the natural sciences that was now applied to the study of human beings. Comte, Durkheim, Weber, Spencer, and Huxley were main contributors as sociology came into its own. Darwin's work was important for establishing an evolutionary perspective on human nature, and Freud's new psychology was on the horizon.

Room needed to be found in the curriculum for the social sciences, and the humanities became squeezed from that direction. The natural sciences, too, exerted pressure, with the federal government adding to it by looking to higher-education institutions for leadership in developing applied science. Among several government programs of financial support was the Morrill Act, which provided for the establishment and maintenance of agricultural and technical colleges throughout the country.

As the humanist tradition struggled to accommodate modern literature and to maintain dignity and strength in the face of the growing stature of scientific studies, it was also confronted by the trend at leading American colleges to repattern themselves as research universities. Several features were borrowed from the German university model, considered by many people to be the innovative leader of its day in Europe. The first American graduate schools appeared during this period (the first arts and sciences programs; professional schools of medicine and law already existed), putting an emphasis on specialization that was passed on to the undergraduate level. Departmentalization and specialized studies became popular, depreciating the notion of a college graduate who had read the great works from many fields. And the elective system arose and spread quickly, with some colleges by the turn of the century having few courses required. As a result, collegewide reading lists were eliminated or considerably thinned.

The twentieth century has followed in the fashion of the latter nineteenth. On the one hand there has been continued expansion of the canon. As the century draws to a close we find that authors like Shaw, Proust, Woolf, Faulkner, Kafka, Camus, Wittgenstein, Heidegger, Sartre, Veblen, Keynes, Mead, Buber, Toynbee, Levi-Strauss, Whitehead, Einstein, Dobzhansky, and many more are taking their places among the greats. On the other hand, the changes that led to scaling down great books study have grown even stronger. And to them has been added another force. There has been a dramatic rise in the level of schooling of our population. From about 10 percent attending high school at the turn of the century, today more than 50 percent go beyond high school to higher learning. With increasing numbers of students has come an increasing emphasis on the social utility of what they learn. While we educate the masses, says this twentieth-century version of the American penchant for practicality, what is best for them is job training and learning basic skills for good citizenship. The great books have increasingly been thought of by many educators, as well as by the general public, as inappropriate for the task, as old, stuffy, inapplicable to the everyday lives most students are preparing for. Whereas practically minded educators in Franklin's day were still respectful of the great books, their latter-day counterparts became less so.

It is not that the canon has been eliminated from the curriculum. Throughout the century most high-school and college students have been exposed to at least a few canonical works, but only a small number have gone beyond this point. In high school, what students typically have read are a few works of literature in their English courses, with *The Odyssey*, *Oedipus Rex*, *Hamlet*, *Othello*, *Ivanhoe*, *The Adventures of Huckleberry Finn*, and *Walden* being some of the favorites of teachers. The last couple of decades have brought this practice under review, and contemporary works have sometimes been substituted, but the anticanon movement that has been influential in higher education has impacted more slowly on high-school English teachers. Reading the classics outside of literature has been less common in high school, although many students have encountered documents like the Declaration of Independence, the U.S. Constitution, and the Gettysburg Address. Works written in languages other than English have been read in translation. The teaching of Greek had for the most part faded away by the turn of the century, as did Latin, except at Catholic schools, around midcentury. (Latin was still popular among college-bound students for the first several decades, but its purpose was to give a foundation in language skills that could be applied to modern languages, rather than preparation for reading the classics.) Many high-school students have studied modern languages, but few have achieved the proficiency needed to read a classic work in one of them.

A few high schools have defied the prevailing trend, and today there are still some that offer substantial reading in great works. There are also some elementary schools that emphasize "junior" great books and follow a canon of age-appropriate readings. (For instance, fourth-graders would read Hans Christian Andersen's "The Emperor's New Clothes," an adaptation of *Ali Baba and the Forty Thieves*, selections from *Alice in Wonderland*, and so on.) Urging from the background is the Great Books Foundation, a national organization that provides reading lists and training for educators, including those who wish to lead study groups outside of school.[22] But in spite of its nationwide reach, this organization has not been embraced by most schools or parents, and it affects relatively few.

In higher education, too, the field of English has been a strong force in preserving the great books, although ironically it is professors of English who have led the recent anticanon movement. For many decades it was common for students to take at least a two-course sequence in the great works of American, British, or "world" (usually meaning European) literature. As general education requirements were relaxed, this practice gave way at most schools to only one course (or sometimes none) in English beyond composition. And the content of the single course has been the topic of intense debate and variation. Those students who decide to major in English are, of course, exposed to a number of canonical works, but few students choose that major.

Philosophy is another field where the great books have been and continue to be a main focus, but, except at Catholic colleges, it has long ceased to be a requirement; hence it reaches far fewer students than English. And even at Catholic schools, where until the 1960s the philosophy requirement was often a half-dozen to a dozen courses, it now is more likely to be one or two.

In history, where we might expect reverence for the great books of the past, the works of the great historians have seldom been read. History courses have employed secondary texts, sometimes supplemented by a classic or two from philosophy or politics to give students a firsthand acquaintance with the period and place under study. But many historians now classify such works as "intellectual history" or "history of ideas" (as opposed to history of events), splitting them away from the main field.

Foreign-language departments have taught many students the basics of modern languages, and a handful have studied Greek or Latin. Second-year language study sometimes includes reading a great work or two, but extensive reading from the classics in their original languages is done only by the few students who take advanced courses.

Political science departments usually offer at least one course in political theory that involves reading the masterworks, and the same goes for the other social sciences, with titles like "History and Systems of Psychology," "Social Theory," and "History of Economic Thought." But again such courses usually are taken by only a few students for their majors or as electives; they are not the standard fare of general education.

In mathematics and the natural sciences, few departments include readings from the classics in their coursework, whether for general-education students or for majors. While college students may express familiarity with names like Euclid, Galileo, Darwin, and Einstein, very few have ever become acquainted with their writings directly, and of those who have, it is likely that they did not do so by taking science courses.

Many, perhaps most, college students today, then, are exposed to at least a few great books, through an English requirement and maybe a course or two they will elect in philosophy, history, or the social sciences. This is a reduced state from earlier in the century, although that time, too, was far from the heyday of the canon. Even Robert Hutchins, one of the century's most noted great books advocates and teachers, admitted that as an undergraduate at Yale he had read only three or four of the long list of works he later taught and promoted.

Few students have asked for an experience different than Hutchins had. While there have been various student causes and movements, advocacy for study of the canon has not been one of them. Among educators, there has continued to be a significant portion who are advocates in heart and mind, but many of them have not cared to oppose the inertia of the twentieth-century curriculum. Attempts to do so have often been unsuccessful, and canon supporters have routinely found themselves on the defensive. Successful attempts to mount an offense have appeared occasionally, but have been isolated from college studies at large. Frequently they have been in the form of specially designed great books programs that have been branded as "experimental" or "alternative education" options to mainstream schooling.

Carrying the torch for the canonists have been such figures as Irving Babbitt of Harvard, who led a "generalist" movement among literature professors at many colleges during the first couple of decades of the century; Alexander Meiklejohn, who established a great books program at the University of Wisconsin in the 1920s; Hutchins, president of the University of Chicago in the 1930s and 1940s, who founded its famous and controversial great books program and was instrumental in establishing the St. John's College (Maryland) program; William Bennett, Chairman of the National Endowment for the Humanities and Secretary of Education during the Reagan administration; and Mortimer Adler, who was a student and teacher at Columbia University during its revival of teaching the great books in the 1920s, designer of Hutchins's Chicago program and his colleague in the St. John's effort as well as in editing *The Great Books of the Western World* (the original edition in 1952 by

Encyclopedia Britannica included fifty-four volumes encompassing seventy-four authors and over four hundred works from various fields, and constituted an influential twentieth-century voice in stipulating the content of the canon), and tireless author, editor, and organizer on behalf of the great books throughout the century to the present. And there have been other notables, too, among them Mark Van Doren, Jacques Barzun, Lynne Cheney, and Allan Bloom, who have spoken on behalf of the great books within academia and beyond.

Today, Meiklejohn's Wisconsin program is long gone, having lasted only a few years, although it inspired a similar short-lived effort at Berkeley in the 1960s. University of Chicago students still read from the great books, but in a much less extensive and more loosely organized program than the one begun by Hutchins. Columbia's program is very much alive, but has undergone several transformations. St. John's, now with a second campus in New Mexico, has become known as *the* great books college, where the full four-year curriculum is devoted to reading from the canon, including the great works of mathematics and science (see Appendix B). Several other small colleges, including Thomas Aquinas (California), Shimer (Illinois), and Magdalen (New Hampshire), offer full great books-based bachelor's degrees, and as many as a few dozen more institutions have programs of a lesser scale but still consisting of at least several courses organized together and involving substantial reading from the canon (often selections rather than entire books). Some of these programs offer the equivalent of a major, others are designed to fulfill general-education requirements, and some are honors programs. In these programs students read the classics of ancient Greece and Rome and of later Western civilization. Often included are a few non-Western works, as well as writings on the presently popular political topics of race, class, and gender. The courses are usually interdisciplinary and the books are read in English translation, as they were written originally in a variety of languages. The usual classroom methodology is small group seminar (sometimes supplemented by lectures) in which students and instructors discuss their interpretations of what has been read, compare and contrast with other works, and debate about the propriety of what the great authors have said. A list of schools (comprehensive, but not claimed to be exhaustive) offering such programs includes Assumption College, Boston College, Boston University, Eckerd College, Franciscan University, Grove City College, Kentucky State University, Kirkwood Community College, Louisiana State University, Lynchburg College, Millsaps College, Mount Saint Mary's College (Maryland), Northwestern State University (Louisiana), Pepperdine University, Providence College, Rhodes College, Reed College, Richland College, Saint Andrews Presbyterian College, Saint Joseph's College (Indiana), Saint Anselm College, Saint Mary's College (California), Saint Olaf College, Saint Thomas University (Florida), Seattle University, Thomas More College, University of Dallas, University of North Carolina at Asheville, University of North Texas, University of Notre Dame, University of San Francisco, University of the South, University of Southern Maine, University of Tennessee at Chattanooga, and University of Texas at El Paso. But with more than three thousand higher-education institutions in the United States, the percentage is small that offer anything more than scattershot acquaintance with the great books through a few randomly available courses.

The rationale that twentieth-century advocates for the canon have used to support their pedagogy is multifold. It echoes our educational heritage back to fifth-century Greece, although one element thereof is not often heard today. The claim that the great books should be read for their own sake gives way to arguments that speak in terms the American penchant for practicality can relate to. Defenders of the canon today usually try to begin on common ground with listeners who demand usefulness from the curriculum.

One favorite argument has been the skills argument, that classic works engage students, more so than other works, in learning to read carefully and thoughtfully and to think critically. A starting point here is the notion that the mind is strengthened mechanically simply by pushing itself hard enough against rigorous material, analogous to the way that lifting weights strengthens the body. But also important is the idea that from the classics the mind draws important content. As Jacques Barzun has put it, the effort of grappling with often-difficult-to-read classics gives us possession of a vast store of vicarious experience; we come face to face with the whole range of perception that mankind has attained and that is denied by our unavoidably artificial existence. Through this experience we escape from the prison cell . . . it is like gaining a second life.[23]

The content or "whole range of perception" consists partly of the basic names, places, events, and dates of cultural literacy, but as Barzun and other canon advocates are quick to note, that substance also includes the great ideas. Those ideas are the main currency highly functioning minds use, and as the Sophists long ago emphasized, students need to learn what the great ideas are if they are to become convincing communicators and successful debaters.

But latter-day canonists are not Sophists. While promoting the skills argument, they have also justified the great books on grounds that sometimes sound Platonic and at other times are reminiscent of the Oratorical-Humanistic tradition. They are concerned that students go beyond Sophistic relativism to locate a proper model of morality, and they believe the content of the canon provides a most important knowledge in this regard. It is knowledge of the most fundamental sort, not of limited use, but broadly applicable. This knowledge constitutes a unity that subsumes the many and often-competing particular ideas included in the canon. In one sense the unity associated with the canon is identified with the foundations of Western culture. The cultural unity argument for the great books sees them as a medium for putting readers in touch with the broad expanse of that culture across times and places. In another sense of unity, the great books are sometimes linked to a philosophy of human nature and human knowledge. The human unity argument looks beyond Western culture to claim that the common core of ideas the books put us in touch with is a defining feature of humanity per se.

As to what constitutes the ideas that speak so fundamentally, canonists sometimes begin by citing "enduring" questions like "What can I know? What should I do? What may I hope for? What is man?"[24] In a more extensive framework, Mortimer Adler has identified 102 topics, such as Beauty, Being, Democracy, Good and Evil,

Justice, Mind, Causation, and Time, and helped to popularize the term "great ideas" to describe them[25] (see Appendix A). The great ideas are multifaceted: about each there are various answers or points of view. The great books present a plurality or diversity of outlooks to be wrestled with. But those outlooks are subsumed within a whole, be it Western culture or human nature and knowledge. Studying the great ideas is seen as following a debate, but one with the ultimate purpose of pointing students in the direction of truth and proper values.

The importance of studying the great books to learn about Western culture has been summed up well by William Bennett: We study Western culture because it is ours and because it is good.[26] On the one hand we recognize that, like it or not, the cultural milieu in which we live is Western, and studying its foundations and monuments is a preparation for living successfully within it. On the other hand we find the very makeup of our own cultural foundations to be preferable to that of other cultures, especially because it developed such features as freedom and democracy. The human unity explanation says that through studying the great books we learn what it is to be human in the fullest and best sense. We come to understand the human essence and what distinguishes it from the various cultural and individual manifestations thereof, what it takes to live life successfully and happily in accord with our species-being.

By universalist standards, what makes a great book great, what accounts for its elevation beyond other books and secures canonical status for it, is its capacity to provoke insights into the great ideas. It does this especially well. While other books may do so to some degree, and some books, whether or not they do, may meet with ephemeral popularity, a great book endures, it stands the test of time and is read in eras beyond the one in which it was written. It endures because the idea(s) it addresses are expansive across time, rather than particular to a given time frame. Similarly a great book's appeal extends beyond geographic locale, nationality, language. People of various backgrounds can profit from it because the great ideas are applicable at least throughout a unity as large as Western culture, and, if the thesis of human unity is accepted, to people everywhere.

Great books, of course, come in differing forms that employ

differing means to get at the great ideas. Some are treatises that present observations or arguments in straightforward fashion. Others are works of imaginative literature: poetry, plays, novels. The former approach the great ideas directly and obviously through the power of reason. Literature, on the other hand, deals in image and symbol, and employs emotion to open the reader's experience beyond the rational faculty. Still, what we draw from such literary experience that makes it so worthwhile that the work causing it is judged to be great has to do with parts of the intellectual terrain circumscribed by the great ideas. The pedagogic importance of great works of literature involves learning to experience symbolism, imagination, emotion, but, further, it involves learning *through* those processes; their operation tells us about something—something that relates to the basic ideas human beings think deeply about and that form the basis for the ways they conduct their lives.

Summary of Part I

The educational practice of teaching the great books has been at the center of the curriculum in Western culture throughout most of its history. Three main justifications for this presence that were announced with its beginnings in ancient Greece are still the main justifications heard in the twentieth century: by studying the canon students develop skills associated with critical thinking; they become immersed in the tradition of the culture in which they are living; they develop an understanding of the universals comprising human nature and providing the basis for all knowledge. These lines of thought prevailed as the canon survived an early debate about the existence of universals and the question about whether they can be learned from books, a medieval challenge that the classics should be discarded because of ideologically incorrect content, the dark ages during which many books were lost either temporarily or permanently, the Enlightenment battle of the books between ancients and moderns, and the early-American penchant for practicality that demanded schooling be immediately and practically useful. Throughout this history the canon continued to grow and be shaped into the form we know today, and at times it was revised to include whole new categories of works: Roman works were added to Greek, modern-language works were added to classical, and the social sciences were added to the humanities and natural sciences.

Beginning more than a century ago in American education, continued cries for practicality, along with pressures from scientific studies and from specialization and electivism, finally overcame the traditional thinking and caused an eclipse of teaching the canon that is in an advanced stage today. At most schools there is only a minimal place in the curriculum for a smattering of great works. A few schools and programs, however, operating out of the mainstream, have kept the tradition alive, and a few prominent educators and promoters have managed to bring it occasional visibility within academia and among the intellectually inclined elements of the general public.

Part II

🪶

ANTICANONISM

A COUPLE OF DECADES AGO, an anticanon movement began to grow in American higher education and it has quickly reached proportions of historic significance. The great books were once again becoming involved in a major controversy. It might seem odd that the canon could command so much attention in an age when its place in the curriculum for most students had already been reduced to a few readings in a required English course and perhaps one or two other courses. But there were certain factors at work that combined to again put the canon in the limelight.

The reputation of the great books was one factor. While carrying the taint of impracticality, they nevertheless continued to be thought of by many people as a distinguishing ornament. While comprising only a small share of a typical student's program, acquaintance with the canon meant a touch of class, a sign of cultural high standing. A college graduate in any field appeared better than the rest if able to demonstrate cultural literacy by being conversant about the great books. While its place in the curriculum was minor, the canon still functioned as an icon of respectability. When it came under an attack that threatened to erase what remained of it, not only did faculty who taught canonical works offer resistance to protect the small turf they had left, but other people took notice as well. Suddenly, something assumed to be part of our heritage, even if not usually paid much attention to, was being maligned, and it became a cause to be defended.

The cause was not an independent one, however. Higher education has been swirling with change, the result of something the opponents of which have described as political correctness and supporters have hailed as multiculturalism. At issue are concerns about admissions criteria for students (past academic performance versus diversity by race, class, and gender), faculty hiring and promotion (again, meritorious performance versus race, class, and gender), the nature and scope of sexual harassment, speech codes outlawing offensive language, and censorship of speakers and promotional literature. Going along with these concerns has been a strong questioning of what students are taught. The curriculum, too, has been under pressure for change by multiculturalism. The canon, in its role as preserver of cultural tradition, has been an obvious target for new ways of social engineering.

Accompanying the new social engineering are recent intellectual forces that have underlain and provided justification for it. The canon as preserver of culture thereby has become not only socially inappropriate, but unacceptable on sophisticated theoretical grounds. Comprising the new intellectual forces are what is often described generically as "postmodernism," allied with certain features of left-wing political thought. The fields of philosophy and especially literary theory have led the way, although other fields have participated as well. Such intellectual approaches as neo-Marxism, structuralism, deconstructionism, hermeneutics, reader-response theory, and feminism have thrust their way into prominence. Figures like Jacques Derrida, Michel Foucault, Roland Barthes, Paul de Man, Jonathan Culler, Edward Said, Terry Eagleton, Jane Tompkins, and Stanley Fish, to name only some, have provided the inspiration and fundamental ideas.

The new forces have reacted against the very basis upon which teaching the great books has traditionally been justified. Anticanonism opposes universalist thinking in both its Platonic and Humanistic forms. The notion that there is a core nature to humanity, or a set of universally human truths and values that we can come to know, is said to be outdated and mistaken. Instead, it is said, knowledge varies necessarily according to the conditions of the knower. One dimension of anticanonism, then, is epistemological. The other dimension is political. In reaction to the practice of passing on our cultural heritage out of reverence for it, and the belief that it provides a proper grounding for the moral aspect of our lives today, it is pointed out that the generally accepted canon is made up of works by European and American authors, nearly all of whom are white and male. Not only do those authors comprise an unfairly chosen elite, but their works that have been lauded as "great" contain messages that reinforce a dominant politics of oppression. The epistemological and political dimensions are often interrelated. Some opponents of the canon may emphasize one or the other, but an understanding of anticanonism's full force involves both epistemology and politics and recognizes their linkage.

The Epistemological Dimension

Anticanonists view the notion of a universally applicable knowledge as a dogmatism. They see what philosophers have often termed "essentialism" or "foundationalism" to be the promotion of a secular scripture, and they reject it as being out of step with contemporary times. They point out that claims about the universality of human nature are passé in the intellectual climate of the latter twentieth century, as are claims about finding a universal wisdom within the books we read.[1]

The antiuniversalist viewpoint emphasizes that knowledge is inescapably context-bound. Its contextual limitations are established by the time, place, and social conditions in which it is conceived. There are no such things as universal truths or values, it is held, although there can be shared meanings within groups of people who are of the same time, place, and conditions. Knowledge of the world is not unitary; rather, there is a plurality of belief systems, each of which works from a different context. The supposed universals that have been so often touted as synonomous with humanity at large are merely the substance of one mindset, not necessarily representative of other mindsets. Roland Barthes identifies the "disease of thinking in essences" with "bourgeois mythology."[2] As Michel Foucault states,

> these notions of human nature, of justice of the realization of the essence of human beings, are all notions and concepts which have been formed within our civilization, within our type of knowledge and our philosophy, and that as a result form part of our class system.[3]

Following this line of thought, we could claim that a plurality of belief systems, besides that of universalism, exists both within our own civilization as well as outside of it. These systems are grounded in ideas other than beauty, being, justice, and so on, or at least define these ideas differently than is done through the intellectual tradition with which the canon has been associated. There is no corner, then, on right knowledge. Knowledge varies among human beings; it is plural and relative to the contexts in which it is conceived.

If universalism is rejected and pluralism reigns, then the beliefs and values of a particular context are subject to rejection or redesign by other contexts. When this circumstance is directed toward the written word, the consequence is that the meaning of any given work stands to vary according to the context from which it is interpreted. This point has been applied to the writings of various fields, although not without difficulty in the empirical sciences. But it has appeared most often and most forcefully concerning works of literature, and sometimes philosophy and history. Consider, for instance, Augustine's *Confessions*. One interpreter may find the work to demonstrate devotion to God, while another interpreter may see the author to be presenting a psychology appropriate for struggling against the status quo. In another example, literary theorist Jane Tompkins, in her now-celebrated discussion of Hawthorne, notes that one critical view of Hawthorne's *Provincial Tales* finds the common theme of the tales to be good versus evil, while another critical view (coming from a different context) finds the theme to be dependence and carelessness versus manly freedom and responsibility.[4]

There are many other examples that might be cited to represent the fact that famous products of language have been subject to differing interpretations. But especially provocative is Stanley Fish's imaginative interpretation of William Blake's poem "The Tyger." One respected critic, we learn, sees the tiger as good, while another respected critic sees it as evil, and still other critics see it as both good and evil or beyond good and evil. Fish outdoes them all by suggesting how the poem might be seen as a description of the human digestive tract.[5] The meaning of the poem, as with the meaning of other works, is thus demonstrated to vary according to the context of the interpreter. Fish is quick to point out that not just anyone can dream up a personal interpretation that is as significant as any other interpretation. There are limitations in this regard. (Presumably the expertise of the interpreter and the detail and comprehensiveness of the interpretation are key factors.) But contextualism does mean to assert that standard interpretations that are assumed by many people to be "right" interpretations of the written word are only relative ones: there is no one "right" interpretation, there are plural interpretations.

The contextual variability of meaning applies regarding the interpretation of canonical works as well as other works: the great books could be interpreted in different ways depending on the context from which one approaches them. This contextual notion of meaning militates against the canon in that if there are different views of what given works mean, determining what ones are great becomes problematic. One interpreter may find a particular work to be highly meaningful concerning philosophy of life, while another reader, coming from a different context, might find the meaning to be different and much less significant. Here we recognize that meaning is closely related to value. The meaning we attach to a work is not synonymous with its value, but meaning and value are collaborative. When a work is found to be highly meaningful, that is, the meaning is recognized to be important, an assertion has been made about value. It is in *valuing* books that contextualism applies most forcefully against the canon.

If, as contextualism holds, universalism is a faulty notion, then establishing a list of books as great because of their portrayals of universals is a faulty approach to evaluating literary works. The value of a book must derive from some other source than its putative connection with universals. As Barbara Herrnstein Smith puts it, "Literary value is radically relative and therefore constantly variable."[6] As Terry Eagleton puts it, "There is no such thing as literature which is 'really' great, or 'really' anything, independently of the ways in which that writing is treated within specific forms of social and institutional life."[7] Books that have acquired greatness within the context of universalist thinking should not be assumed to hold such lofty status when judged from other contexts. Other contexts can be expected to see things differently. Plurality means difference. A plurality of contexts for judging written works suggests that there will be a plurality of judgments about which works are of most worth. The fundamental ideas that predominate in traditional Western culture, and are often mistakenly thought to be universally applicable to humanity per se, are not the ideas fundamental to other contexts within or outside of that culture. Those other contexts have their own predominant ideas, and based on such will suggest a different list of books that are to be preferred. The notion of a universal canon that bridges local contexts is discarded along with the notion that there are universal ideas that such a canon portrays. This point is stated clearly in a document sponsored by the American Council of Learned Societies:

> The very possibility of a "canon" under these circumstances becomes questionable. Should we not insist, rather, on the necessity of reading works in relation to other works of their traditions and thus resist the idea of a more comprehensive canon, countering it with a series of deeper, more locally-articulate studies?[8]

Following this line of thought, we would find that works by the likes of Plato, Sophocles, Aquinas, Shakespeare, and Milton, which are accepted as canonical within the context of traditional Western culture, may give way to other works preferred in other contexts.

When this idea is applied directly to the curriculum in our colleges, one result is that reading lists controlled by the canon are judged to be highly restrictive. Professors come from differing contexts, and those whose contexts are nontraditional find noncanonical reading materials more appropriate for their students than the standard great books. To stay with the canon, forcing it upon teachers to convey to their students, seems inappropriate if the value of reading any given book has no grounding in universality. Without exposure to a plurality of contexts, students will fail to broaden their horizons, fail to see the breadth of intellectual terrain available in the world. They will not develop the critical perspective that comes from trying on different contexts and then viewing other contexts from those vantage points. They will lack a heightened sense of critical thinking.

Further, we must remember that the relativity of the value of a book is related to the relativity of its meaning. Professors, then, will no longer want to convey to their students the notion that interpreting the written word is a matter of searching for hidden but fixed messages. Students will have picked up this universalist notion from their elementary and secondary teachers, but professors enlightened by contemporary literary theory find it not simply irrelevant, but pernicious. It gives students a wrong picture of the basis for the linguistic element of life; it is an idea they should be disabused of. They need to come to appreciate contextualism, and approach reading in terms of it. When no longer fettered by devotion to universalist thinking, they will be able to explore traditional as well as nontraditional works with an imaginative force that befits critical thinking.

To sum up the epistemological dimension of anticanonism, it is antiuniversalist. Knowledge, it is held, does not admit of universals; rather, knowledge is contextual, relative. Books do not convey universal knowledge, since there is no such thing. And there are no universally great books: judgments about greatness are relative to the contexts within which they are made. All of this points toward rejection of the traditional curriculum for its adherence to canonical readings, and for failing to open students' minds to contextualism.

The Political Dimension

While some anticanonists are willing to leave their complaints about the canon at this general level of epistemology, many others go further. They see recognition of the contextual nature of knowledge, and of the relative worth of any book, as only the initial step in understanding the problems attendant with a great books-oriented curriculum. A second step involves asking what is the nature of "context," and what specific contexts can be identified? If context is all important, an understanding of its makeup is needed.

Eagleton, as we saw, identifies contexts with "specific forms of social and institutional life," Barthes finds the context of essences to be "bourgeois," and Foucault relates context to "class system." Stanley Fish holds that the standards of value that shape the canon are the product of "historical, political, and social" forces,[9] and that the relevant factors are "the accidents of class, race, gender, and political circumstance."[10] To locate the various elements of context under a generic label, it is often said by anticanonists that context is political. The term "political" has become a common shorthand. That is, a person's political status is seen as determining what knowledge that person considers to be of most worth and what books the person considers to be most significant.

Knowledge is found to be saturated with politics. When the traditional Western canon is seen to be the product of a certain context, that context is designated to be political in nature. So, too, are other contexts recognized to be political in nature, and the fact that a plurality of political contexts can be identified is often accompanied by the claim that the canon represents a particular political position among others. The position the canon is said to represent is that of conservativism: the content of the vaunted great books is reputed to be the stuff of conservative thinking. Anticanon politics cast this position in negative terms: the canon is criticized as an instrument for political oppression, for keeping a certain elite group in power at the expense of other people.

In *The Politics of Literature*, a leading primer of dissent against the canon, Sheila Delany presents this perspective forcefully:

But the premise—that a literary training can help conservative consciousness—is not mistaken, for the masterpieces of English and American literature have usually supported conservative values: the sanctity of private property, the inevitability of social class, women's natural inferiority, and an otherworldly rationale for the way things are. The lines quoted earlier . . . represent a cultural norm: the loyalty of most literature to ruling-class values of its time.[11]

Delany's specific reference is to Anglo-American literature (novels, plays, poetry), but anticanonists often apply her point to a more extended version of the canon: works of various fields and by authors of various European nationalities. And to her citation of women and the class-bound oppressed, racial minorities are added to round out the list of persons under domination. The expression "class, race, and gender" employed by Fish (not to imply that he coined it) has become synonomous in current anticanonist parlance with "political." If the term "political" has come to characterize the nature of context, then "class, race, and gender" (the order of the words is often changed, and of late the popular expression is "race, class, and gender") has become the rallying cry that characterizes the meaning of political. Race is used loosely to include certain ethnic minorities (Hispanic, for instance), although often blacks are spoken of to exemplify this category; and class can include non-Western peoples colonized by Europe and America. Other popular terminology includes "marginalized groups" to describe collectively women, racial minorities, and the class-bound, and "hegemony" to describe their status as being dominated by an elite of white males of European and American heritage. Reading the traditionally established great books is seen as an exercise in becoming indoctrinated in status quo thinking, which is apologetic for the maintenance of power by that elite. Marginalized groups are found to be portrayed by canonical authors as subservient, and as if their condition is natural or at least not improper or challenged.

Typically cited examples of the message of oppression attributed to the canon are Aristotle's apology for the institution of slavery in his *Politics* and his view of the inferiority of women found in the

Poetics, Dante's advocacy of kingship, Milton's biblical account in
Paradise Lost of Eve's indebtedness to Adam for her very creation,
Gibbon's disparagement of Moslems, Twain's demeaning portrayal of
blacks in *Tom Sawyer* and *Huckleberry Finn*, and James Fenimore
Cooper's suggestion of the propriety of separation of the races. And
there are many other examples, including less obvious ones than
these, that are revealed by the machinery of recent sophisticated
approaches in the analysis of literature.

Revealing the function of canonical works as instruments of
political oppression highlights the elitism of the canon. The desig-
nation "great," when applied as it has been traditionally to certain
books, now means those books are suspect. They are part and parcel
of high culture, which is considered to be antipopulist, anti-
egalitarian. "High culture," say Louis Kampf and Paul Lauter in their
introduction to *The Politics of Literature*, "propagates the values of
those who rule and therefore helps to maintain current social arrangements."[12] The monuments of literature are not objects of
reverence for anticanonists; they are viewed uncharitably as reser-
voirs of outmoded values. While canonists approach the great books
with veneration, and are not mindful of those books collectively
presenting a particular political point of view, anticanonists confront the same books with denigration because they are perceived to
be shot through with retrograde right-wing politics.

The content or subject matter contained in the great books,
then, is disparaged by the political dimension of anticanonism. A
second component of the political dimension begins by asking, Who
are the authors of the canon and what are the mechanics of canonization? Anticanonists often challenge canon advocates to name female, minority, and non-Western authors whose works appear on
lists of the greats. Few such names are forthcoming. The few that are
usually mentioned are female poets and novelists of the nineteenth
and twentieth centuries, such as Emily Dickinson, Jane Austen,
George Eliot, the Brontës, and Flannery O'Connor. The overwhelming majority of authors whose works are heralded for greatness
are Western white males.

This fact about the authorship of the canon leads anticanonists
to the charge that the process of canon formation is political in

nature, and to complaints about that condition being both unfair and educationally unacceptable. Authors other than Western white males, it is said, have been victimized by discriminatory circumstances. And when their works fail to appear on great books lists, readers who concentrate on those lists lack exposure to key ideas and perspectives that authors other than Western white males have to offer. Further, those readers lack exposure to a diversity of authorial role models.

Anticanonism rejects the universalist claim that the great books stand the test of time because they deal with universal ideas; substituted instead is the notion that context determines claims to greatness. When context is defined as political, then so, too, are claims to greatness. Works and authors that have become canonized are revealed as beneficiaries of political forces working in their behalf. Tompkins asserts this position strongly:

> a literary reputation could never be anything but political . . . works that have attained the status of classic, and are therefore believed to embody universal values, are in fact embodying only the interests of whatever parties or factions are responsible for maintaining them in their preeminent position . . . the literary works that now make up the canon do so because the groups that have an investment in them are culturally the most influential.[13]

One of the two factors typically cited in the politics of making literary reputations is having connections with powerful people. Some authors benefit from the patronage of influential friends and business agents, while other authors have no such advantage. Tompkins's study of Hawthorne notes that the original promoters of his works included the already-famous Longfellow (Hawthorne's college roommate) and publisher James T. Fields. Their counterparts today who make and maintain reputations are not only the publishers who continue to reprint Hawthorne's works, but the army of experts (college professors, librarians, and so on) who carry on the tradition of reverence for the author. Tompkins contrasts Hawthorne with Susan Warner, who wrote at the same time he did.

While her works did not go unpublished or unrecognized, she did not have the influential contacts of her counterpart, and, it is imputed, her reputation thus suffered for posterity.

The cases of Warner and Hawthorne are meant to exemplify the unfairness that women have experienced at the hands of the canon makers. A similar complaint could be lodged in behalf of minority authors. Traditionally, those who have benefited from access to the power brokers of culture have been white males; women and minorities have been largely lacking that access. This disparity bespeaks unfairness, and suggests that there may be worthy works by women and minorities that have been relegated to oblivion. Lacking patronage, the authors failed to reach the threshold of greatness, and history has passed them by.

This characterization of canonization continues. Once an author or work has been canonized, it is said, greatness adheres thereafter. While the ideas and values by which literature is judged may change from one era to another, each era will find its own reasons for continuing to revere what posterity has told it is a monument. The canon is fluid in the sense that authors and works are added as new ones appear and initial reputations are established. And reputations can fluctuate over time, sometimes rising and declining on several occasions through decades and centuries. While a rise thrusts a name or title to the fore, a decline is not enough to eliminate it. As one critic has said about American poets,

> We rarely exclude a poet completely once he has been included for any length of time. A reputation may fluctuate wildly, but it will rarely collapse. Once in, a poet tends to stay in, if only in a small corner of the attic.[14]

To employ a different image, the canon could be thought of as growing like a museum collection. Only a limited number of pieces will be on display at any given time, and just what those pieces are will answer to currently popular trends, but many pieces that are not on display remain in the collection.

And just as popularity trends influence what works are on display at a given time, those trends also influence what works become part of the collection in the first place. Besides patronage, the other main factor many anticanonists emphasize in the politics of making a literary reputation is whether an author strikes a chord in dealing with dominant ideas and values. Female and minority authors, it is pointed out, often speak in different voices, ones that run counter to the canon's political conservativism. Scholars who critique female-authored literature and black-authored literature often express the view that much or most of what these literatures have to say locates them outside of the traditional canon. Terms like "female perspective" and "black tradition" are employed to describe the distinctness of these literatures, although there has been confusion and disagreement over just what constitutes such a perspective or tradition. Sandra Gilbert and Susan Gubar speak of "the many ways in which women poets and fiction writers have confronted female experiences of creation and procreation, marriage and maternity, adolescence, aging, desire and death,"[15] and assert that "the striking coherence we noticed in literature by women could be explained by a common female impulse to struggle free from social and literary confinement."[16] Henry Louis Gates, Jr. traces the "black tradition" in literature to the autobiographical "deliverance" narratives of slaves and former slaves, and tells us that "the inscription of the black voice in Western literatures has preserved those very cultural differences to be imitated and revised in a separate Western literary tradition of black difference."[17] The different voices of female and black authors are seen typically to relate to the conditions of oppression blacks and women have experienced at the hands of white males. While this factor is found to be present in various ways and degrees, it is sensed as a unifying thread within literature by women and literature by blacks. Since white males have comprised the cultural establishment that bestows canonization, writings by women and minority authors that reveal conditions of oppression by those white males are perceived as a threat to the establishment. Such writings certainly have gotten published, and some have been widely read. But, the argument goes, by and large they are too great a threat to the white male power structure to be recognized as great and afforded a position of literary immortality.

To use another term, the it is the "otherness" of female and minority writings, contrasted with what stands as mainstream writings, that prevents their reaching great books lists. Works by non-Western authors, anticanonists note, are also thrust into the domain of "otherness," with the same result. Non-Western authors are absent from the canon because it has been defined traditionally as a product of Western culture. European-American thinking identifies a common cultural heritage that it wishes to pass on to future generations of Westerners as embodying their roots. Non-Western, by definition, is "other," foreign to the basis of our cultural unity. And by virtue of its being "other," its quality or value is diminished. Non-Western is often judged to be inferior, to be less desirable than Western. Anticanonists see the West-as-best perspective as analogous to the dominance of white males over females and minorities. The "other" is cast as inferior; the literature of the "other" does not meet canonist standards because it fails to resonate the thinking of the West. The charge, then, is gross ethnocentrism, a narrow-minded sense of superiority about self.

The "otherness" of non-Western works is, of course, greater in variety than that of Western female or black writings. There are several major cultural traditions to be accounted for, and a time frame dating to antiquity. But works as diverse as the *Bhagavad Gita*, the poetry of Li Po, and the *Koran* are seen as sharing a differentness that comes from being other than Western. Further, there are the works of postcolonial non-Western authors, many of whom focus upon their legacies of oppression at the hands of a powerful elite: white European male colonists. Here is a close kinship with the Western "female perspective" and "black tradition," as the factor of class (economic and social) occupies the stage with gender and race. Western females and blacks share with non-Western colonized peoples a degraded status and suffering caused by the same oppressors. These voices speak in unison about the condition of servitude and struggle to break free. Scholars from the newly developing field of postcolonial studies criticize the canon in a likewise fashion with their Western cohorts in oppression, and are sometimes thought to speak for the epitome of the "otherness" that canon makers reject.

While there is a strong feeling among anticanonists that the canon's dearth of works by other than white Western males demon-strates unfair treatment of the excluded authors, the greatest con-cern is not for authors but for readers. Complaints about the politics of canonization focus especially on pedagogical matters: how readers of the traditional canon are being limited, what they are missing out on. One complaint, voiced by a mild strain of canon criticism, says that readers of the traditional canon are missing out on developing the sort of awareness that will be essential for them to live suc-cessfully in the twenty-first century. Women and minorities are moving toward equal status, and class boundaries are becoming fuzzier and less inhibiting. Many non-Westerners are now living in the West and especially in the United States, and the United States has increasing dependence on its economic and political connec-tions with non-Western nations. Heterogeneity prevails, diversity is the new order. Students must learn to respect the differentnesses of previously marginalized groups. If they concentrate on reading the works of traditional white male Western authors, and consequently fail to become acquainted with the different voices that nontradi-tional authors offer, they will lack the perspective needed to under-stand and cope in tomorrow's world.

Most of the more prominent anticanonists prefer a stronger line of criticism. The world may be changing, they would say, but we have a long way to go before it is in good shape. The pragmatic concern that students learn to adjust to their environment is super-seded by a demand that they develop a critical judgment for identify-ing what is wrong with it and understanding that it is still in need of remaking. By not being exposed to the different voices of nontradi-tional authors, students will lack a key opportunity to become sensi-tized about the forms of oppression that not only characterize our past but are still embedded in our social and cultural fabric today. The desire is that students come to understand the plight of women, minorities, and the class-bound oppressed: white males need to learn to appreciate the degraded and unfair status of people unlike them-selves, and those of one oppressed group need to learn of their kinship with (and differences from) those of other oppressed groups. All students, then, would benefit from exposure to diverse and countercultural ways of thinking. They would learn political awareness that moves them together in one direction. But the traditional canon stands as a monolith disallowing any politics besides its conservativism.

Still another perspective within the pedagogical concerns of anticanonism deemphasizes learning to understand people of other backgrounds, and also deemphasizes sharing a political direction with them. Rather than, or more important than, understanding other types of people is an emphasis on understanding oneself. In order to achieve self-awareness, and develop a sense of personal identity, it is said, students from marginalized groups must confront their oppressed status and work through it. Particularly noteworthy as an inspiration for this line of thinking are the views of psychiatrist Frantz Fanon on life under colonialism. He asserts that the major weapon of colonizers is to impress an image of inferiority upon the people they oppress, and that it is imperative for the oppressed to shed this image if they are to successfully reach freedom and equality.[18] Applying this line of thought beyond colonialism to other forms of oppression as well, anticanonists have decried the canon for failing to offer female and black students the "female perspective" and "black tradition" that are crucial for working through the images of self that they have inherited from traditional culture. These students are not simply being denied exposure to political diversity when they are immersed in the canon, but they are denied an opportunity to find their true identities, to develop fully as woman or as black. For proper psychological development, then, students from marginalized groups are seen to need a reading list that emphasizes countercultural, that is, countercanonical, works on race, gender, and class.

Rounding out this self-identity argument is the point that a critical factor in breaking through a negative self-image, and achieving a confidence attendant with freedom, is exposure to the right role models. One source of such exposure can be fictional or historical persons who are written about in books. But another most important source is knowing about the authors of the books one reads. Students who are fed a diet of traditional canonical works will get the impression that great writing is done by Western white males. The absence of authors of other backgrounds makes a strong statement that implies those authors lack the capability to write great works. Students from marginalized groups will assume that they themselves have lesser capability, and their achievement will thereby suffer. The problem of reading influencing self-identity, then, is not just that the canon fails to include nontraditional ideas because it fails to include the nontraditional authors who put forth those ideas. The problem is also the fact that the absence of non-traditional authors from the canon conveys an oppressive idea in itself. As a corrective, giving students a diet of readings whose substance allows them to identify with their gender or race is not enough. There needs to be an emphasis on those readings as being written *by* the groups whose conditions the readers are trying to relate to.

To sum up anticanonism's political dimension, it finds epistemological contexts to be saturated with politics, the most important categories of which are race, class, and gender. The canon, it is said, represents the politics of conservativism: in its content, minorities, women, the class-bound oppressed, and non-Western peoples are portrayed as inferior; and in its selection process they have faced overwhelmingly discriminatory conditions. A canon-centered curriculum is rejected for not acquainting students with the multicontextual nature of our contemporary world, for indoctrinating them with conservative politics rather than opening their minds to its oppressiveness, and for disallowing students of marginalized groups a key opportunity to work through their oppression psychologically and achieve proper personal identities.

Anticanonism's Alternative Curriculum

Anticanonism's epistemological dimension, its position that the greatness of a book is a false idol determined by context rather than inherent qualities, opens the way for a curriculum built around new goals and inclusive of nontraditional readings. One technique for rejecting tradition is to emphasize that instead of reading "literature," students will encounter "texts," since the latter term avoids a connotation of judgment about greatness. Theoretically, this democratic approach to reading might include any linguistic formulation that has been recorded, as Robert Scholes informs in his statement that "No *text* is so trivial as to be outside the bounds of humanistic study. The meanist graffito, if fully understood in its context, can be a treasure of human expressiveness."[19] An anticanon reading list, then, will include a variety of writings that are representative of differing contexts. Scholes and two colleagues have published a text following this principle: "By substituting the concept of *text* for the traditional concept of *literature*, we accomplish a number of things. We allow for the presentation of a wider range of material and a broader spectrum of approaches to literary study."[20] Appropriately, the book is entitled *Textbook*. Its content includes numerous short selections, and some are from well-known figures like Ezra Pound, W. H. Auden, Sigmund Freud, William Carlos Williams, John Milton, James Joyce, William Shakespeare, Ralph Ellison, and the brothers Grimm. But these selections are afforded no more credibility than those written by lesser lights, including a United Press International press release, advertisements from Nike athletic shoes, Prudential Life Insurance, Visa International Hotels, and an Aristotelian assessment of television commercials.

The purpose of exposing students to such a diverse set of readings is not to have them brush against greatness and absorb some of it. The notion of greatness has been replaced by that of context. But what do students learn from exposure to a variety of contexts? The answer, put in generic terms, is critical thinking. Students are taught to dig into the contexts the works they read represent, to appreciate the complexity of language and how meanings are variable and relative. This is the overall message underlying the epistemological dimension of anticanonism, and *Textbook* is designed to introduce students to it. It represents well a sentiment being voiced by many college and university faculty who are engaged in redesigning the curriculum. The Syracuse University English Department, for instance, in a collectively written manifesto, has stated that "the end of an education in literature will be, not the traditional 'well read' student, but a student capable of critique: of actively pressuring, resisting and questioning cultural texts."[21]

When this aim of anticanonism's alternative curriculum is

understood, the political dimension can be found in close accompaniment with the epistemological. When it comes to critiquing texts and culture, many anticanonists are not satisfied with simply having students develop an incisive mind and do so by reading just any text. There are certain features of our cultural tradition—the political ones of race, class, and gender—that are to be given emphasis, and there are certain kinds of reading materials that are especially relevant in this regard. If students are to learn to be critical of race, class, and gender as traditionally found in our culture, they need to read materials that will suggest a critical position to them. And it is important that a substantial number of those materials be written by members of oppressed groups, so as to provide proper role models for students who are themselves members of those groups. In some cases politically motivated anticanon curriculum design still leaves a portion of the reading list for canonical works, but counters them with a generous amount of reading from the new politics. In other cases canonical works are left out entirely (or nearly so), or are included only if they are deemed to relate favorably to the new politics—the works of Marx, for instance.

A good example of the political dimension of anticanonism's approach to curriculum design can be found in the highly publicized curriculum revision at Stanford University in 1988. Before this time, all students were required to take three courses (on a quarter system calendar) in which they would read a core of books from the traditional canon. Afterwards the requirement of three courses remained, but only a handful of "Common Readings": Marx, Freud, the *Bible*, and some broad designations such as "a Classical Greek philosopher," "an Enlightenment thinker." A new statement of purpose became effective, along with eight "tracks" or reading lists from which students choose one. Written into the general objectives of the program (covering all tracks) was the requirement "to further understanding of self, others, and society and therefore to confront issues relating to class, ethnicity, race, religion, gender and sexual orientation, and to include the study of works by women, minorities, and persons of color." The instructional objectives then included: "to promote awareness of cultural assumptions and values and their historical or contemporary relevance by exposing students to criticisms of and alternatives to these assumptions and values," and "to give substantial attention to the issues of *race, gender, class,* during each academic quarter."[22]

After the revision, some tracks continued to be much like traditional great books programs, with the addition here and there of works such as Sappho's poetry, the *Koran,* Christine de Pizan's *The Book of the City of Ladies,* and Toni Morrison's *The Beloved* to ensure minimum compliance with the new objectives. Other tracks embraced the new objectives much more openly and fully; they demonstrate what a carefully prepared politically motivated anticanonist curriculum looks like. The Philosophy track in the 1990–91 academic year (see Appendix B) included standard canonical works by Homer, Plato, Aquinas, Descartes, Erasmus, Shakespeare, Hume, Galileo, Kant, Marx, Adam Smith, Freud, Kierkegaard, and others. But fully half of the readings were presentations of liberationist ways of thinking about race, class, and gender, largely by contemporary authors, and many by females and minorities. A partial list includes "Aristotle and Women" by Horowitz, "Fathering the Unthinkable: Masculinity, Scientists, and the Nuclear Arms Race" by Brian Easlea, *Coming Into Being Among the Australian Aborigines* by Ashley Montague, Frederick Douglass's autobiography, Mary Wollstonecraft's *Vindication of the Rights of Woman, Incidents in the Life of a Slave Girl* by Harriet A. Jacobs, "Origin of the Confederacy of Five Nations" by C. H. Henning, "Ethno-Archaeology of the Florida Seminole" by Charles H. Fairbanks, Simone de Beauvoir's *The Second Sex,* "Political Philosophies of Women's Liberation" by Alison Jaggar, *The History of Sexuality* volume I by Foucault, *Racial Hygiene* by Robert Proctor, *The Interpretation of Cultures* by Clifford Geertz, *Ideology* by Plamenatz, "Chief Seattle's Message," and "Only Justice Can Stop a Curse" by Alice Walker.[23]

Many of these works would be unfamiliar even to most philosophy professors. The reason for their inclusion in the curriculum is their force in presenting a message that counters what is found in the traditional canon. The latter can be exposed as classist, racist, and sexist, and the culture it represents demonstrated to be passé, to be in need of replacement with contemporary ways based on new perspectives on equality and justice. The content of these works tells us such directly, and their authorship by people of marginalized groups says so boldly, if indirectly. The canonical works that are read function as a negative backdrop for contemporary thinking that presents a political message that does justice to traditionally marginalized groups. The political message becomes the driving force behind the curriculum; presenting it to students is the primary objective.

In this example of an anticanon curriculum, then, students do read canonical works, or perhaps better said, they confront those works and question them and the culture they represent. Such a confrontation allows contextualism to shear canonical works of their reputations and expose them as mere texts, and at the same time demonstrate how those reputations are consistent with certain elements in our culture that are held to be undesirable.

Perhaps it would be objected that this interpretation exaggerates how a reading list combining canonical and noncanonical works is actually used. It might be said that students are asked to read all works open-mindedly and to draw their own conclusions about which ideas to accept and which to reject. And after all, one of the main canonist arguments in favor of reading the great books is that ideas can collide with one another and be sorted out. Such is the approach of literary theorist Gerald Graff, a leading figure in the canon debate who early in his career was supportive of canonism, but in recent years has promoted the view that we should "teach the conflicts." Graff's position is the central thesis behind two books he has authored,[24] and he has promoted it at academic conferences, as a consultant, and through articles in prominent academic journals. Other scholars have picked up on "teach the conflicts," and suggestions have been made to institutionalize that strategy.

What Graff proposes is to make the debate over the canon the backbone of the curriculum, with both sides in the debate given recognition as having legitimacy. Students would come to understand much better than they do now the tensions between certain of their professors that impact on determining what books and ideas will predominate in the curriculum. And the curriculum itself would reflect the overall state of affairs, or collective wisdom of conflict, that constitutes the reality of intellectual affairs among academics today.

One of Graff's favorite examples is his own teaching of Conrad's *Heart of Darkness*. Students read the work itself, and traditional commentaries about it, and then for a counterview they read Chinua Achebe's *Things Fall Apart*, along with other contemporary writers who deal with racism and colonialism. This leads to a discussion of the influence of politics on literature, especially the question of whether literature is inevitably political. In sum, Graff says, "I now teach *Heart of Darkness* as part of a critical debate about how politics and power affect the way we read literature."[25]

Graff's position has sometimes seemed appealing to open-minded canon supporters. On closer examination, it is seen to be one of the more subtle versions of anticanonism, since what it does is give that perspective a major portion of the curriculum. It is unclear whether Graff intends that each traditional great book students read should be paired off against a nontraditional book, but the gist of his statements leads in that direction. Neither does he state specifically that the "conflicts" he has in mind are only those of race, class, and gender. But again his statements and examples seem to lean that way. "Teaching the conflicts" can easily turn out to be something like Stanford's philosophy track. When half of the reading list concentrates on the particular issues of race, class, and gender, even if those issues are presented as material for open-minded debate, the course students are taking has been heavily weighted by one aspect of the intellectual landscape. That is, even if students are not encouraged to accept a particular political position, the framework for debate the curriculum presents leads them to conceive of traditional Western culture and its canon especially or primarily in terms of race, class, and gender, and to see nontraditional works as equipment for interrogating the tradition on those terms.

If balancing canonical works with noncanonical ones represents the subtle side of anticanon curriculum design, there are other cases where the weighting is even more pronounced, and the reading lists bear few or no vestiges of the canon. Consider the First-Year Program at St. Lawrence University. All students enter residential colleges where they take two courses (one each semester) that constitute the core of their general education. The courses differ, with each college designing its own, but overall only a few canonical works are evident, and in many courses they are nowhere to be seen. The overwhelming emphasis is on leftist politics as taught through contemporary works. The fall 1993 syllabus of Campbell College (see Appendix B) focused on autobiography, with its purpose to "investigate the intersecting issues of race, class, gender, spirituality, and nature." The reading list consisted of *Pilgrim at Tinker Creek* by Annie Dillard, *Black Elk Speaks* by Black Elk, *I Know Why the Caged Bird Sings* by Maya Angelou, *This Boy's Life* by Tobias Wolff, *Woman Warrior* by Maxine Hong Kingston, *Writer's Inc.* by Sebranek et al., and a xeroxed reader with such selections as "Elvis for Everyone," two lectures by the Dalai Lama, "American Indian Autobiography," and "Conspicuous Consumption."[26] The second-semester follow-up course concentrated on "the first-person narratives of individuals whose issues and struggles may resemble our own," as well as

> experiences that some of us may not have encountered first-hand, such as prison life, AIDS, homelessness, sexual violence, and lifeways among subcultures of gays and lesbians. We will study and apply critical approaches to the process and politics of constructing a Self and an Other.

The required readings were essays and first-person texts, with those by the most recognizable authors being "If Men Could Menstruate" by Gloria Steinem, "Harlemite" by Malcolm X, "Stranger in the Village" by James Baldwin, and "Men's Bodies, Men's Selves" by John Updike. None of the readings were from the traditional canon, and all were from the latter twentieth century.

Many of St. Lawrence's First-Year courses make extensive use of films, and Gaines College in the spring of 1994 offered a full course on films that address

> social forces such as the breakdown of the community, the increasing disparity between the rich and the poor, the expansion of bureaucratic capitalism . . . with cultural forms such as the American Dream . . . and the rhetoric of freedom and equal opportunity.

The films studied were *The Graduate, Grand Canyon, Brewster Mc-Cloud, Apocalypse Now, Full Metal Jacket, Taxi Driver, Husbands and Wives, She's Gotta Have It, Thelma and Louise, Suburbia, Paris, Texas, Wild at Heart, Down By Law,* and *Raising Arizona.* An alternative course entitled "Rock 'n Research" concentrated on "political and social issues" as seen through American popular music, primarily rock and roll. Required texts were *Facing the Music, Present Tense: Rock & Roll and Culture, On Record: Rock, Pop, and the Written Word,* and *Rolling Stone Illustrated History of Rock and Roll.*

The idea that films and musical compositions qualify as texts is not unique to anticanonism. Canonists might easily agree, noting that many great written works have been made into films and that some original films are becoming classics, and citing music from classical to jazz as relating important ideas to be reckoned with. While canonists would not recommend the substitution of these arts for reading the great books, they might (and in some great books programs do) integrate film and music with reading lists. What is anticanonist about the St. Lawrence film and music courses, as well as that institution's other First-Year courses and their equivalents at other institutions, is the set of ideas that the texts are meant to deal with. The subject matter is race, class, and gender, and the perspective through which it is approached is that of recent left-wing politics, which are placed in opposition to the rest of the Western and American tradition.

Limitations and Errors of Anticanonism

In challenging the very grounding that supports great books study, anticanonism becomes an important force to be reckoned with. It points to traditional support for the canon as epistemologically and politically smug, and moves canonists to examine principles they may have accepted uncritically and thought to be unassailably given: about knowing universals and finding them in books, about the greatness of books being based on qualities in the books themselves, about the propriety of the messages found in canonical works.

Anticanonism, then, acts in a positive way as a gadfly to keep canonists on their toes. But the attack on the canon is not possessed of a substantiality that should allow it to unseat or outlast dedication to study of the great books. Anticanonism is fraught with difficulties: its claims are one-sided and excessive.

Logical Dilemma

One of the most obvious of the difficulties is a simple matter of logic. The antiuniversalist contextualism that forms the basis of anticanon epistemology redounds upon itself; it is, if not inconsistent, at least limiting in its self-referentiality. The claim that knowledge is inexorably context-bound is itself a knowledge claim, but what happens when it is assessed as such? By its own standards it can be no more than another context-bound claim. It cannot be asserted in universalist terms, only in contextual ones. If one goes beyond this limitation and does assert that contextualism holds universally, then clearly an inconsistency occurs: the claim that knowledge is contextual (there are no universals) is defied by the acceptance of a universal (the claim that there are no universals). Contextualism does not allow itself to be established on firm ground.

But what if one is faithful to the limitation, trying to hold consistently that contextualism is no more than one among other positions that could be held within other contexts? Surely this position can be seen as unsatisfying: what reason is there to accept a contextualist context over a universalist one? If contextualism admits of the limitation it places upon itself, then the cause to accept contextualism becomes problematic. The difficulty here is a version of or akin to the paradox of skepticism that has amused philosophers for many centuries. If a skeptic claims that there is no such thing as truth, it seems that this claim in itself is a truth claim, and it thus refutes itself. If the skeptic softens the claim and avers that the skeptical position on truth, too, is uncertain, then justification for accepting it over other positions on truth becomes problematic.

Confusion about Multiple Meanings

Still, let us suppose that in spite of contextualism's difficulty in justifying itself logically as a general principle, one is still committed to the idea that knowledge is context-bound. Further problems arise when this principle is applied to cast doubt on the meaning and valuation of literature. Contextualism claims that the meanings of books vary according to the contexts of their readers, that books are interpreted differently in different contexts. Given such differences, canonical works cannot be claimed legitimately to provide knowledge of universals. The fact of differing interpretations leads to the conclusion that we cannot find universals in literature. Support for this view lies in the many examples that could be cited, such as Fish's about "The Tyger." But the fact that multiple interpretations exist need not lead to the conclusion that universalism is a chimerical notion. About some books there may be genuine differences of interpretation, even among experts. And, seemingly, a clever alternative interpretation could be devised for any book by stretching the imagination far enough (witness Fish). But there are counterexamples that can be noted in defense of universalism. Is there a reasonable and intelligent reader who would not recognize that *Antony and Cleopatra* is about the tension between the fulfillment of erotic desire and the achievement of political ambition? The work can be read in various ways, emphasizing one or another element found in it, but can this basic meaning be denied? Consider Keats's "In drear-nighted December." Is there a reasonable doubt that whatever else might be said of it, it is about the pain of romantic love?[27] The strategy of citing examples, then, can be employed not only by contextualists, but by universalists, with the latter pointing out that many works have clearly identifiable basic meanings that can be understood and shared across contexts. While meaning is sometimes and in some ways variable, at other times and in a fundamental way, it is transcontextual.

This position, of course, relies on the conception of a "reasonable" reader, a conception that might be challenged by contextualists. But they would be hard-pressed to deny that transcontextual meanings exist, that there are certain meanings that celebrated books have carried to readers over time and across languages and national boundaries. As a further and final example here, although many others could be given, consider Aristophanes' play *The Frogs*. Written in ancient Greece, it has been read by readers of various centuries, languages, nationalities, customs, and so on, and experts still find room to debate certain points about its meaning. But readers of all times and places have found in it the basic meaning of the clash of old versus new values. Although the context(s) from which readers today approach this work will be far from that of its author, they get the gist of its basic meaning. Contextualists favoring leftist politics understand this basic meaning just as do readers who fail to share their epistemological or political leanings. A reader who fails to admit to this basic meaning is one who can fairly be said to be lacking in reasonable understanding.

Contextualism's force is mitigated by recognizing that trans-contextual meanings do exist, and that in at least some works they are obvious. But the contextualist point remains true as well—that about many works there has been debate, even among experts, over interpretation. A further response is needed to the contextualist argument that pointing out differing interpretations leads to the conclusion that we cannot find universals in literature. Having questioned the premise of the argument, we turn to the inference through which the premise is linked to the conclusion. From the premise that different critics find different meanings in a given book, that is, the critics differ regarding the supposed universals they find the book to relate to, it does not follow necessarily that the book fails to speak to a universalist knowledge. It may very well be that the book is complex and speaks to more than one universal. A great book should not be thought to be limited to dealing with a single theme or dispensing a single message. Given a plurality of themes or messages—one or some more popular at one time and within one context, another or others more popular at another time and in another context—a great book may speak to all of them. Its complexity may be a factor that contributes to its greatness. Consider Jane Tompkins's example of multiple interpretations of Hawthorne's *Provincial Tales*[28] (one interpretation finding the tales' common theme to be good versus evil and another interpretation finding it to be dependence and carelessness versus manly freedom and responsibility). Or consider the example of Augustine's *Confessions*[29] (one interpreter emphasizing the author's devotion to God while another interpreter finds a struggle against the status quo). The works in question may deal with both interpretations, although that suggestion need not be assumed to mean that all identifiable meanings are equally weighted, or that any work deals with any idea any interpreter asserts it does. The suggestion is that multiple interpretations may mean complexity, not that such complexity is evenly distributed or that it might approach infinite proportions.

Mistaken Notion about the Unity of the Canon

Another difficulty with anticanonism is its notion that reading the great books is an exercise in the indoctrination of conservative politics. The canon does not present a unified view at all, politically conservative or otherwise. And reading from its contents, unless done in an unnaturally selective and closed-minded fashion, provokes thoughtfulness rather than indoctrination. Anticanonism is wrong in its basic assumption about the content of the canon, and may also harbor a misunderstanding of how the process of reading the great books contributes to a unified knowledge, or is thought by canonists to do so.

Given the relativity of meaning that the epistemological dimension of anticanonism espouses, it would seem inconsistent to then assume that the great books are purveyors of a particular point of view, that they present the specific meanings associated with political conservatism. The political dimension is at odds here with the epistemological, at least for those anticanonists who advocate both, as many do. Contextualists would seem to lapse into an epistemology they find fault with canon supporters for holding.

But just what process is involved—or is thought to be by canon supporters, if not assumed to be by anticanonism's political dimension—when readers confront canonical works? That is, how does the process yield a unified knowledge? How do readers come to know universals? It is not the case that a great book *contains* a universal that is then *imprinted* on the mind of a reader. A book is not a conduit through which a universal passes. Universals lie beyond individual minds and beyond containment in printed matter, although mind and print may connect with them. Great books are challenges, invitations to stretch one's mind to grapple with difficult topics and questions. The books present us with meanings, but readers are free to accept or reject the meanings. Good teachers of canonical works use exposure to those meanings as a way of opening discussion of them. Discussion is facilitated by the fact that diverse and contrary points of view are to be found in the canon. In reading a canonical work that deals with the topic of justice, the reader is invited to consider one perspective on that universal, but may end up more critical of that perspective than accepting of it. Other canonical works will present other perspectives. An understanding of justice is approached only gradually, as a variety of perspectives is considered. Books may be reread and perspectives revisited with readers changing their minds and expanding their understanding of what justice entails. Far from it being the case that a hard and fast meaning of justice is imbued on a reader, it is instead readers who are active in interrogating canonical works and wrestling with the meanings they encounter there.

The process of reading a great book and approaching knowledge of a universal might be likened to walking a pathway that leads through a landscape to be viewed. That landscape, in turn, is merely part of a vast terrain made up of many, often-interconnecting, landscapes. Other walks along the same pathway may provide sights not discovered the first time, and other pathways into the same landscape will provide fascinating contrasting perspectives of it. Each landscape is complex, and can be appreciated only with much effort and by returning again and again via various pathways. Viewing and appreciating the whole terrain is a lifetime pursuit, and one that even then cannot be accomplished fully, but only to a degree. Still, as viewers continue to return, taking familiar paths as well as unfamiliar ones, they develop fuller and more refined visions of what they have seen.

This description of the process involved in coming to a knowledge of universals through reading the great books suggests that such a knowledge is available, but the canon, as a vehicle for approaching it, is not unified but diverse. That anticanonism does not recognize or admit this diversity, and instead sees the canon as ideological, as a bastion of political conservatism, is perhaps its most glaring fault. To locate the difficulties with this political characterization of the canon, it will be helpful to recall the earlier-cited quotation from Delany:

> But the premise—that a literary training can help conservative consciousness—is not mistaken, for the masterpieces of English and American literature have usually supported conservative values: the sanctity of private property, the inevitability of social class, women's natural inferiority, and an otherworldly rationale for the way things are. The lines quoted earlier . . . represent a cultural norm: the loyalty of most literature to ruling-class values of its time.[30]

Delany, it was noted, seems to be referring specifically to the field of study today defined by the term "literature" (novels, plays, poetry). But here again, as with the claim that contextualism is supported by the fact of multiple interpretations, the point is carried by anti-canonists to apply to other fields as well. Their rhetoric is often imprecise, and their disparagement of the canon lumps together any great works of the past, without specifying that in some fields there are great works that have little, if anything, to say of a political nature. Descartes' *Meditations*, Hume's *Inquiry Concerning Human Understanding*, and Kant's *Critique of Pure Reason*, are good examples in philosophy, as are Bacon's *Novum Organum*, Copernicus's *Revolutions*, and Newton's *Principia* in science and mathematics. The universals that the great books give us access to include many that are not political. From Adler's list of 102 great ideas, just some of the nonpolitical ones include animal, cause, change, element, logic, mechanics, medicine, one and many, space, time, universal and particular. It is a mistake to dismiss the great books as an instrument of conservativism, then, first for the reason that those books have much to say that is not political.

Still, much of what they have to say does focus squarely on political matters (defined broadly to include the factors Delany cites: property, class, women, and otherworldly rationale). This is what novels and plays, works of history, religion and many from philosophy and the social sciences are all about. They are didactic: they present identifiable political messages and invite readers to accept them. It is the didacticism of the great books that critics are worried about.

But where the critics are mistaken is in failing to recognize or admit that the political messages found in the canon are not unified, but instead are plural, and often competitive with and contrary to one another. Conservative politics can be found in the canon, but so can politics of other sorts. Reading the great books does not imbue students with any particular viewpoint, but exposes their minds to a plurality of them. Some teachers may slant their teaching of canonical works toward conservativism (through a narrow selection of books to be read or through the way they interpret the books), but the opposite potential is there as well: to slant great books pedagogy toward left-wing thinking. The books themselves, however, do not contain a unitary political doctrine, and if taught in a representative cross section, they will convey no such doctrine.

It was noted earlier that support for the critics' charge that the canon is saturated with conservativism comes largely by means of citing examples. An effective rebuttal to the charge also makes use of examples. Sometimes a plurality of views can be found within a single work. In the *Canterbury Tales*, "The Wife of Bath's Tale" extols the sovereignty of women in marriage, while "The Clerk's Tale" and "The Merchant's Tale" preach the opposite, and "The Franklin's Tale" describes a marriage of mutual sovereignty and obedience. In the *Bible* the idea of punishment appears often, with the three main philosophies of punishment we still debate about today all well represented: retribution, prevention, and reforming the wrongdoer.

While examples of this sort are not uncommon, for the most part the contrast of ideas present in the canon emerges *between*, rather than *within*, various works. The great books contain various points of view concerning property, class, women, and other-worldly rationale. *Wealth of Nations* supports capitalism, but is countered by *The Communist Manifesto*. Many novels offer subtle or overt support for social and economic classism, but they are balanced by works by Dickens, Hugo, Sinclair, Steinbeck, and others. Political tracts by Aquinas and Dante favor monarchy; Aristotle and Burke speak for oligarchy; Paine's writings and the founding documents of the United States (*The Federalist Papers*, the Constitution, the Declaration of Independence) are the literature of government by the people.

Augustine and Aquinas depreciate woman as compared with man (à la Genesis), Schopenhauer and Nietzsche are openly derisive of women, and other works are more subtly sexist. Still, *The Republic* promotes equality for women, as does J. S. Mill's *The Subjection of Women*. In *Lysistrata*, women organize to control men. Novels like *Pride and Prejudice* and *The Mill on the Floss*, while not strongly feminist by today's standards, show women in their struggle with the mores of male dominance in the eras in which they were written. Ibsen's *A Doll's House* is well known as a feminist play. And then there are the works of Mary Wollstonecraft, Virginia Woolf, Simone de Beauvoir, and others that are in the process of becoming canonized and becoming standard fare on college reading lists. The great books are not mired in one-sided sexist dogma.

About "an otherworldly rationale for the way things are," again Delany's perspective overgeneralizes. Sophocles' Oedipus plays tell of the folly of human defiance of a higher order, and Homer does the same, as do the *Bible* and many great works of the classical and medieval eras. Later works like Pope's *Essay on Man* emphasize that humanity should remain within its limits. But Renaissance humanism signals a trend toward glorifying human potential, the nineteenth-century Romantics seek human access to the infinite (consider Keats's *Endymion*, Shelley's *Prometheus Unbound*), Nietzsche proclaims boldly that God is dead, and Sartre's works echo this theme.

The list could go on and on, including many other works, and many themes besides the four dealt with here. But the few examples mentioned serve to illustrate that the canon is quite pluralistic in viewpoint. Many of its works were intended to criticize and offer alternatives to the social, political, and religious beliefs and institutions of the times in which they were written. And many of them have a similarly stimulating effect today. Perhaps this is most evident when we read humorous and satirical pieces like those of Chaucer, Rabelais, Boccaccio, Erasmus, Voltaire, and Fielding. We are not only entertained by their cleverly devised incidents and irreverent gibes, but we are stirred to take a critical look at "establishment" values in our own time.

It is an ironic fate for the great books that they are misunderstood as purveying conservativism, when, in fact, it is through these books that many people, prior to the latest generation, became enchanted with communism, social equality, sexual equality, and antireligious sentiment. That irony is reinforced by the fact that during the 1950s, when many great books reading groups were popping up at libraries around the country, librarians wanted reassurance that the books would not anger patriotic and religious groups.[31] The canon that critics today portray as too right-wing was, just a few decades ago, suspected for being too left-wing.

Overemphasis on Politics in Canon Formation

The point that many canonical works were originally written to be critical of the cultural climates in which their authors lived provides the beginning of a rebuttal to the anticanonist position that the process of canon formation is predominantly political. One of the two main political factors claimed to be at work in bestowing greatness on authors is that their works are in step with their times, reflective of the dominant attitudes and values; works like those of female and minority writers are denied a fair hearing because they are critical of the status quo.

It may be that holding a political position opposed to one's dominant culture has in some cases deterred the achievement of greatness. But there are obvious cases where it has not. Chaucer, Rabelais, and Voltaire spoke against the dominant cultural climates of their times, yet their works have achieved canonical status just the same. In fact, the antiestablishment tenor of those works seems to have had a reverse effect from that of deterring greatness: it has been a favorable factor contributing to their success. *Gargantua and Pantagruel* and *Candide*, for instance, speak in highly irreverent fashion about various forms of prejudice and abuse. Readers in the times they were written appreciated them as exemplars of protest, just as readers do today. The protest shouts out across the centuries, and demonstrates that canonical works survive the test of time because what they have to say has universal appeal.

Consider, too, the example of Rousseau's *Discourse on the Sciences and the Arts* (often remembered simply as "The First Discourse"). Critical of the classical and medieval tradition that was his heritage, and critical as well of the ideas of his contemporaries, Rousseau won the prestigious essay competition at the Academy of Dijon in 1750. The author dispraised the academic establishment of his day, but was still acclaimed by it. Later in his career the publication of *Emile* (particularly the section on "The Creed of the Savoyard Priest") drew denunciation from the Catholic church, and the author left France to ensure his safety. But his message about religion was not thereby stifled, and, if anything, was enhanced in the eyes of many readers. Rousseau's writings, like those of Rabelais, Voltaire, and many others, possess intrinsic merit that shows through in spite of a dominant politics they oppose, and they actually feed off from that opposition. While not all antiestablishment authors fare as well as the ones mentioned here, it is easy to see that celebrity has been afforded to brilliant literary efforts that buck the system, and that it is too facile and general an answer to say that the mistreatment of authors in the process of canon formation stems from their expression of countercultural messages. Other causes should be sought.

The anticanonist assessment of canon formation, of course, does cite another cause: the connections certain authors have initially with powerful people and institutions, and the continued aura of greatness that accompanies a book through time once it has made a name for itself. To sum up the argument, patronage issues reputation, and reputation is self-sustaining; patronage is often unfair and reputations are often undeserved.

This line of thinking, too, fails to give adequate credit to the intrinsic merit of a great work. Theorists like Tompkins do not deny that a book may have a worthwhile content, but they see patronage as the overwhelming reason for the success of one book versus another. Surely this is a lopsided characterization of what makes a great book great. It may be that an author has benefitted initially from patronage, but if a work is to stand the test of time, a test that means it will be assessed by critics (including professors and editors) holding various and contradictory predispositions toward it or what it stands for, it must be possessed of a marvelous substance. In spite of what Tompkins and company assert, critics do not simply follow the crowd in accepting a given work as great and then come up with contemporary reasons in support of it. Rather, judgments are demanding and harsh, and a work must demonstrate intrinsic merit deserving of continued approval, and not rely mainly on the fact that it once was popular.

An example from the visual arts may serve well here, since judgments by critics in that arena, too, are often accused of being politically motivated. The creation of Michelangelo's artwork in the Sistine Chapel was supported by patronage, and since its creation it has been marveled at by many viewers. Its reputation has lasted not because Michelangelo had patrons who created a mystique that viewers of the Sistine Chapel then for centuries followed out of reverence. Rather, it is because this work of art is magnificently crafted and is a moving portrayal of various elements of Christian doctrine and the ideal of unity. It is true that the artist, and this work as well as others done by him, benefited from the influence of people with power and wealth. But how many other paintings are there in existence, done by other artists, that are as magnificent and moving?

A great work stands on its own merit regardless of the system of patronage that may have contributed to its reputation. This point holds not only for paintings, but for masterworks of all sorts, including those of the written word. What will anticanonists say, we may wonder, if Alice Walker's The Color Purple continues to be as visible as it has been for the last few years on college reading lists, and it reaches the point of being generally regarded as having achieved canonical status? Will canon critics pan it for being the recipient of patronage, and depreciate its intrinsic merit? Or will they continue to see it as a compelling portrait of the injustice black women have faced in American society, and justify its inclusion in the canon on that basis?

It might be tempting for anticanonists to claim that Walker's book, and other highly visible ones by women and minorities protesting injustice, have avoided the baggage and taint of patronage; that the message they convey, rather than preferential treatment of their authors, is the reason for their acclaim; that they are breaking down the corrupt system of canon formation and achieving greatness on sheer merit, whereas other canonized works have relied heavily on a system of patronage. But such a characterization will not work. Today's literary climate is quite congenial to works like Walker's. Writings that decry racism, sexism, and classism are promoted by powerbrokers in the literature industry. Faculty appointments and grants, citing the desire to encourage "diversity" or "multiculturalism," often openly favor persons who teach and critique such writings. Certain professional associations have been formed or transformed to concentrate on promoting the writings of women and minorities, and on the analysis of literature from left-wing perspectives. The Toni Morrison Society, for instance, was formed by a group of scholars from the American Literature Association. And according to a recent comprehensive survey, the prestigious Modern Language Association has moved gradually from the practice of publishing few ideological articles in earlier decades of this century to publishing a number of ideological articles in the past decade, the overwhelming percentage of them leftist.[32] Various publishers, recognizing a growing market for leftist writings, have actively sought manuscripts of that sort. Writings are being put into print, critiqued, and placed on student reading lists through a system that parallels the one anticanonists oppose because it smacks of patronage.

Anticanonists who are willing to face up to the fact that they have become the beneficiaries of patronage might then be led to consider whether patronage per se is really wrong, and whether it is possible to avoid it. Is it wrong that an author has benefactors to ensure that a manuscript gets into print and thus has a chance to achieve acclaim? How else does a manuscript come to be printed other than that some publisher chooses it, and in so doing promotes it? How else does a published work eventually come to acclaim other than by having admiring readers? How else does a book come to roost on student reading lists other than by experts giving it their endorsement? Now that anticanonists are establishment-connected, they may come to view patronage in a different light. They may come to see it for what it is: a starting point, secured in various places by authors of various persuasions, that launches their works into the competitive arena where they will have to stand on their own merits if they are to last.

Insubstantial Connection between Anticanon Epistemology and Politics

The contextualist position holds that the values that shape the canon are relative to political forces, and that because of this relativity there can be no such thing as a universally great book. At the same time many contextualists disparage the traditional canon for imparting a particular politics, that of conservativism, which they decry as classist, sexist, and racist. But, we must ask, upon what basis does the disparagement rest? If anticanonists prefer leftist politics, what foundation is there for this preference over a preference for conservative politics? Having disavowed universalism, anticanonism must live up to the fact that it has undercut the strength of its own politics. The most anticanonism can say without overstepping its own parameters is that someone who works from within its particular politics will disparage the canon. What cannot be justified is a claim that this sort of politics is better than another sort. Such a claim would need to appeal to principles that hold transcontextually or universally.

The difficulty being described here for contextualism is exhibited in the work of Derrida. He has taken stands on such issues as neocolonialism, women's liberation, and apartheid, yet his contextualist epistemology leaves all politics ineffable: he has no justification for projecting the rightness of his politics beyond the context in which they were conceived.[33] And regarding the reading of canonical works, Derrida's epistemology would lead us to the conclusion that preferences for determinations about the value of a book are contextual, yet in "The Politics of Friendship" he recommends reading "the great philosophical and canonical discourses on friendship," namely works by Aristotle, Montaigne, Nietzsche, Schmitt, Heidegger, and Blanchot.[34] He recommends reading them from a deconstructionist point of view, that is, from the version of contextualism he is known for popularizing, but what should be recognized is that he has made a choice of works that he believes helpful in comprehending friendship. If he means only that a certain point of view on friendship can be gained by his suggested reading of these works, then he has not overstepped the bounds of contextualism. But if he wishes to argue the transcontextual rightness of the comprehension of friendship to be had in reading his preferred list, he has no ground to stand on. The point here applies to other anticanonists as well. Having disavowed universals, they still take political stands and have preferences for certain books. Book preferences may be for ones that express a particular politics outright, or for works that are to be deconstructed in order to endorse that point of view. In any event, the choice of politics and of preferred reading materials has naught to recommend it; the choice stands on the infirm relativist ground of contextualism. If standards of judgment are relative, then judgments made based on those standards are relative also. As literary theorist Gerald Graff once stated (at a time when he supported the canonist position),

> We are inclined to view the relativity of belief as a liberalizing strategy because it dissolves the authority of dogmatic and totalitarian systems of thought. But this strategy at the same time dissolves the authority of anything that tries to resist these systems.[35]

The declarative politics of anticanonism are undercut by contextualism's lack of grounding for value judgments. But anticanonists hold to their politics just the same, and often seem to want those politics to be viewed not only as right within the context from which they were devised, but as applicable in such a way as to demonstrate the faultiness of other contexts. When it is held by anticanonists that capitalism, racism, and sexism are wrong, that the exploitative practices of the past were abhorrent, as are those that remain today in our society and in others, the assertion is not meant in merely relative terms; it assumes a universality. Even as avowed a contextualist as Eagleton recognizes that the reason for a person becoming a socialist is that "one objects to the fact that the great majority of men and women in history have led lives of suffering and degradation, and believes that this may conceivably be altered in the future."[36]

Eagleton's insight here demonstrates the implicit need of his brand of politics for a stronger foundation than contextualism provides. He does not mean, and neither do other anticanonists who assert similar political views, that exploitation and human degradation can be renounced by a context that is merely one among others. The claim is that exploitation and degradation are wrong per se, that they are now and always have been wrong wherever found. Otherwise, denunciations of the inhumanity that can be pointed to in historical fact and canonical works would be hollow. But the denunciations are not meant to be hollow. The politics that anticanonists assert need and harbor a set of universals that their epistemology refuses to admit to. They need those universals to justify the preference of their own context over other contexts.

The insubstantial epistemological basis of anticanonism for its political preferences also works itself out in another way. Not only is contextualism lacking the authority for declaring anticanonism's politics as superior to others; it is also lacking a necessary connection with such a politics at all. It seems to have been accepted by many anticanonists, and to be the impression that journalistic coverage has given in the debate over the canon, that a denial of universalism links up naturally with leftist politics and with an attendant criticism of Western culture and its canon. It is often thought that if and when a contextualist declares a politics, it will be of this sort. The flip side of this notion is that universalism aligns with political conservatism and with support for the pedagogical tradition of the great books.

The impression that such linkages are hard-fast has been strengthened by the fact that certain high-profile anticanonists have buttressed their politics by railing against universalism, while well-known conservatives have championed the cause of the great books. Fish, Tompkins, and Herrnstein Smith are examples of the former, and William Bennett and Allan Bloom of the latter. But what is missing in this schema is the recognition that the linkages are not necessary ones; their contradictories are just as logical, and, in fact, are not only held by certain contemporary intellectuals but were also held in the past by authors from the canonical tradition itself. Acceptance of the narrow and mistaken schema demonstrates the unfortunate consequences that can accrue to intellectualizing that fails to take adequate account of the history and philosophy available in our tradition.

There is a highly developed strain of political theory tracing from Edmund Burke in the eighteenth century through Michael Oakeshott in the twentieth century that begins with a premise of contextualism but draws a conclusion of conservativism. The idea is that there are no political universals; therefore we should stick closely to the culture that has evolved for us historically. It is the best chance we have, the grounding that prevents confusion and chaos. Change in that culture should be careful and slow so as not to weaken its basic fabric. Followers of this position thus have good reason to favor introducing students to the main elements of the history of the Western culture in which they are living, including its great books.

Contextualism, then, does not necessarily align with the political left. But, further, when it does align in that way it need not deny the importance of cultural unity and of teaching the canon. Take the case of Richard Rorty. He has combined positions of contextualism and left-wing politics, yet still has favored giving students a general education that introduces them to the main elements (past and present) of the tradition that surrounds them. Rorty, whose claims against universalism have often been interpreted by anticanonists as support for their own views, and as akin to inspirations from Derrida and Foucault, has surprised many of his admirers. He has gone on record on several occasions as endorsing the Western cultural tradition (and the American extension of it) and advising that students should read about it through the great books.[37] His reasoning is similar to that of his conservative counterparts on the necessity of recognizing a unity that ties together people's disparate interests.

Moving from contextualist supporters of Western culture and the traditional canon, we turn to universalists who defy the notion that they should be political conservatives. One of Burke's great eighteenth-century adversaries was Thomas Paine. It was Paine from the radical left who spoke of universal human rights and who fomented revolution by the underclasses not only in America, but also in Europe. Paine recognized clearly that a politics of antioppression is strengthened by attaching it to a universalist base that asserts nature as guaranteeing freedom to those to whom it has been denied.

In the twentieth century we find that left-wing universalism aligns easily with study of the canon. We need only to think of Hutchins and Adler, two of the most important figures in the history of the great books movement. Known for touting the great ideas as the ultimate foundation of our knowledge, they have often been assumed to represent conservativism in politics. In fact, however, Hutchins was a New Deal Democrat who after his presidency at the University of Chicago finished out his career at liberal think tanks. And Adler, at least in recent years, has staked out a political position he describes as "socialist" because he finds that human nature and the rights deriving from it support the sort of equality socialism stands for. While some of Adler's critics would find his self-proclaimed socialism overstated and suspect, they would have to find Irving Howe's claim to the same to be impeccable. One of the deans of American literary criticism and of socialist theory, he spoke out against detractors of the canon. Sensing the need for students to get beyond identification with an immediate category such as race, he proposed that they read the great books in a search for basic norms common to all humanity.[38] While Howe did not establish precisely what those norms are, he saw them as connected with the great books and as foundational to successful living through a proper politics.

In short, a contextualist epistemology can link up with conservative politics or with leftist politics, and the same holds for a universalist epistemology. A conservative politics typically aligns with study of the great books. Anticanonists, on the other hand, apply contextualist leftism to rail against the canon, but it should not be forgotten that there are leftists of both the contextualist and universalist varieties who have found their politics consistent with support for the great books.

Summary of Part II

The recent anticanon movement has its philosophical grounding in contextualist epistemology and certain elements of left-wing politics. The epistemological dimension claims that knowledge and meaning are necessarily relative to the contexts from which they are conceived. There are no universals, as evidenced in the fact that books are subject to various interpretations. The political dimension identifies contexts as strongly political, and emphasizes the factors of race, class, and gender. The great books are said to be "great" only as seen from the context of traditional Western culture, which is exposed as a bastion of political conservativism. Anticanonists denounce the content of the great books as indoctrinating students with conservativism, and thus as contributing to the oppression of marginalized groups (minorities, women, and the lower classes). The process of canon formation is said to be unfair to marginalized authors. They are excluded because they lack patronage from the dominant power brokers of culture, and because their writings present messages that are critical of the dominant ideas and values. Students who concentrate on reading the canon are seen to miss out on much-needed nontraditional ideas that would challenge political conservativism, and also to miss out on the nontraditional authorial role models they need to realize that marginalized groups are capable of great authorship.

Anticanon curriculum efforts aim at teaching epistemological contextualism and political leftism. Some reading lists include both canonical and noncanonical works, the former to be exposed as less than their reputations deserve and as political anachronisms, the latter acting as the means of exposure and the presentation of more correct thinking. Other lists ignore canonical works, concentrating instead on teaching left-wing politics (especially on race, class, and gender) through contemporary writings.

Anticanonism is faulty in many ways. (1) Contextualist epistemology, assessed by the terms of its own logic, is self-limiting. Its force is merely contextual and not universal. (2) Contextualism fails to acknowledge obvious transcontextual meanings, and fails to see that multiple interpretations of a book may mean it deals with multiple universals rather than that it fails to speak to a universalist knowledge. (3) The canon is not a repository of political conservativism. Students who read the great books are exposed to a variety of messages: many of them are not political, and while some of the political ones support conservativism, others do not. (4) While the politics of patronage and dominant ideas do influence the process of canon formation, anticanonists have greatly exaggerated the effect. The intrinsic merit of a book is important, and antiestablishment authors and ideas have often made it into the canon on this basis. Further, left-wing writings on race, class, and gender have become establishment-connected and they, too, are now benefiting from patronage. (5) The connection between the epistemological and political dimensions is an uneasy one. Contextualism rails against universals and against the notion of a "great" book, but anticanonists still take political stands that are obviously meant to hold universally, and still recommend books espousing their own favored politics. It should be recognized not only that anticanon leftist politics seem to assume the existence of certain universals, but that both leftism and conservativism can be connected with either contextualism or universalism. And, not only conservativism, but leftism of both the contextualist and universalist varieties, can align in favor of studying the great books.

Part III

🐾

CANON REVISION

W<small>HILE THERE IS MUCH WRONG</small> with anticanonism, reaction to it among canon supporters has varied. Some have trumpeted the pitfalls of anticanonism and defended traditional great books reading lists against encroachment by female, minority, and non-Western authors. It is this side of the canonist reaction, what I will call "strict" canonism, that is most highly visible. But there is another side as well, one that is often obscured by the fireworks that result from a clash of strict canonism with anticanonism. This other side, which I will call "reform" canonism, has spoken out against excessive attacks on the great books, but at the same time has taken to heart the general point made by anticanonism that there are lackings in traditional canonical lists. Reformists have offered plans for limited types of canon revision, and debated with colleagues who oppose it. There are good reasons in favor of revision of this sort, although not all of them have been well articulated. They are grounded in the three basic arguments for teaching the canon that were identified in Part I: (1) the plurality of the canon promotes critical thinking; (2) the canon encompasses a cultural heritage from which students can derive stability and pride; and (3) studying the canon leads toward an understanding of the nature of humanity and the most important elements of knowledge that apply specieswide. A good deal of the discussion surrounding canon revision has concentrated on the plurality factor, although the less frequently heard points about canon revision strengthening unity, at both the cultural level and the wider human level, are especially important ones.

Strict Canonism and Reform Canonism

Strict canonists reject the call for canon revision by appealing to factors of practicality and principle. There is not enough time, it is said, to acquaint students with the great books of our traditional Western cultural heritage, no less to go beyond that heritage. But if there were time, there are other reasons for restricting study to the traditional canon. The argument about time is heard not only from faculty at institutions where students take only one or two courses in which they read from the canon, but also from some of the most extensive great books programs such as the one at St. John's College. Dean Eva Brann states that "we have already pruned and curtailed our works past respectability and cannot find significant stretches for additions." By this perspective, a full four years of college study of the great books leaves no room for bringing in works from outside of the tradition. But, she adds, "if we had a fifth year we might well decide to read some contemporary works of emergent stature. More likely we would try to read in the classics of India and China: The Upanishads and the Bhagavad-Gita, Lao Tse and Confucius."[1] In keeping with this point, the St. John's New Mexico campus has begun a graduate program centered on such non-Western classics as these. But the undergraduate reading list at both St. John's campuses remains entirely Western.

Brann's comments not only remind us of the extensiveness of the traditional canon and the fact that undergraduate reading lists drawn from it must leave out important works. We also note the distinction that canonists (both strict and reform) often make, when dealing with the question of canon revision, between non-Western works and Western ones that are still outside of the tradition. The latter are usually contemporary, but sometimes include works by nonliving women and minorities. Anticanonists sometimes recognize the distinction, but they tend to disregard it, preferring to consider excluded works in general as victims of discrimination. Canon supporters not only recognize the distinction, but also build it into separate arguments.

The works by and about women and minorities that anticanonists want to make standard reading are unacceptable to strict canonists because those works have not met the test of greatness. It is admitted that women and minorities throughout most of history were not allowed formal education equaling that of white males. But the conclusion drawn, rather than the anticanonist one that we should make up for the past by restructuring reading lists to include female and minority authors, is that we cannot change historical fact. Because of past discrimination in the social structure, women and minorities were not equipped to write great works and did not do so. There is a firm refusal to add readings by historically marginalized groups out of sympathy for their marginalized status. Any additions to the canon, it is held, must meet the test of greatness.

Contemporary female and minority authors have not been denied formal education as their historical counterparts were, and some of them may have produced works of excellence. However, they have not stood the test of time: they have not been found by succeeding generations to speak in voices that will extend across centuries to represent the greatest intellectual accomplishments of humanity. There is a longstanding benchmark, tracing to the Roman poet Horace, that requires the passage of one hundred years to make a classic. More recently, canonists have thought in terms of half of that figure, but the point is that before a work can truly be established as great it must become distanced from its immediate surroundings and stand on its own. Strict canonists note that the works by contemporary female and minority writers that are currently popular are largely social protest statements. It is feared that they will eventually prove to have been of ephemeral interest—flashy and emotionally charged, but not of the depth and substance that make for greatness.

The argument is not that females and minorities cannot write great books; even the strictest of canonists admit they can. The St.

John's reading list, in fact, includes Jane Austen, Virginia Woolf, and Flannery O'Connor. They have met the test of time (O'Connor only marginally), and their elevation to canonicity, it is held, has been based purely on the merit of what they say, and with disregard for other factors. But for very many more authors of previously marginalized groups to make the grade, it will take time for the historically new equal-opportunity education of the latter twentieth century to lay the groundwork that will result in canonicity many decades later.

When it comes to non-Western works, strict canonists take a different approach in arguing against adding them to student reading lists. It is clearly not the case that there is a dearth of great non-Western works, or of well-educated authors to write them. Many could be identified, and they span a sweep of time even greater than the nearly three thousand years of the Western tradition. The problem, it is said, lies in the differentness of the non-West. The languages in which the great non-Western books were written are virtually unknown not only to our students, but to our professors as well. This chasm between languages means that the chance of our understanding such works is remote. And it is unreasonable to expect American students and scholars to devote themselves to the many hours necessary to begin to understand Sanskrit, Chinese, and so on. Although this argument is subject to an obvious rebuttal, it has been made in print by such prominent canonists as Leo Strauss and Jacques Barzun, as well as Eva Brann and others.[2]

The difference between the West and non-West, however, extends beyond the realm of language to the related and broader realm of ideas. We read great books to become acquainted with great ideas, and for strict canonism the heart of the problem with reading non-Western works is that their contents are seen to be so very different than the contents of the works of our own tradition. Mortimer Adler makes this point forcefully in stating that

the basic ideas and issues of our *one* Western intellectual tradition are *not* the basic ideas and issues of the *four* or *five* intellectual traditions of the Far East. In the distant future there may be a single, worldwide cultural community with one set of common basic ideas and issues; but until that comes into existence, becoming a generally educated human being in the West involves understanding the basic ideas and issues that abound in the intellectual tradition to which one is heir either by the place of one's birth or by immigration to the West.[3]

This argument relies on the cohesiveness that can be identified among the considerable diversity of viewpoints found within the Western tradition. However extensive that diversity is, and Adler certainly believes it is extensive, he sees it to be superseded by a greater diversity, a global diversity of major cultures. Whereas anticanonists see the embracement of global diversity and an attempt to learn about other cultures as desirable, strict canonists cite it as an impediment that will be ill-understood and likely confuse students trying to make sense of the already large expanse of Western culture.

While strict canonism hunkers down against the idea of canon revision, the reform version of canonism embraces it. Works by rediscovered female and minority writers, highly rated contemporary works, and non-Western works are added to or blended into great books reading lists. There is considerable difference, however, between the reform canonist approach to revising book lists and the anticanonist approach. The difference lies in the degree of revision, as well as in the reasons behind it that become the aims of the professors doing the teaching and that are conveyed subtly or overtly to students. Reform canonists call for a few insertions into lists that remain essentially traditional, as opposed to the wholesale addition and substitution of nontraditional readings. Whereas anticanonists approach the remaining canonical works as mere pieces of communication to be interpreted as one wishes, or as a foil against which the political preferences of nontraditional works are seen to win out, the reform canonist approach still venerates the traditional works and simply attempts to further round out the fullness and greatness of their collectivity.

In presenting the position now of reformism, I will be making the case for what I believe is the proper solution to the canon controversy. At times I will be summarizing views I have heard from other reformists and at times I will strike out on my own, recognizing that even among reformists there are differences of degree and areas of emphasis.

The idea that no time can be found for undergraduates to read outside of the traditional canon sounds much like the plea we sometimes hear from devoted workers and family members that there is not enough time in the day or week for leisure or community service projects or healthful exercise. The answer is that, hard as it may be to take away from what already seems to be stretched thin, adjustments can be made if one is convinced they are important. A number of reform-minded canonists at institutions throughout the country have been quietly going about the business of adding a few nontraditional works to their reading lists, often at the expense of leaving off a few traditional works that would otherwise be included. There are at least two reasons for the quietness of this sort of change, one being that tinkering with reading lists, or what might be called fine tuning, is considered to be standard procedure in good teaching. Good instructors have always done it and will continue to do it, without debate or fanfare. They resist being drawn into the canon controversy because they prefer to devote themselves to the more worthwhile enterprise of teaching. Another reason they want to avoid the controversy is that they do not want to get caught in a cross fire between anticanonism and strict canonism, being perceived from one direction as making only a feeble pretense of change when radical restructuring is demanded, and from the other direction as surrendering to the radical agenda.

The process of canon revision can be found both in departmentally based courses like Introduction to Literature or History of Philosophy, and, perhaps surprisingly to many people, in great books programs as well. The process is also reflected in well-known published collections of canonical writings. While St. John's, applying a strict criterion of greatness, includes only three female authors on its four-year reading list, Thomas Aquinas College lists two (Jane Austen and Edna St. Vincent Millay), and the 1990 revised edition of *The Great Books of the Western World* (edited by Adler) lists four (Austen, George Eliot, Willa Cather, and Virginia Woolf) among its sixty-volume set containing 130 authors, other forums now include works not only by females but by minority and non-

Western authors, and recent works espousing nontraditional ideas. Notre Dame, in a three-year program comprising several courses, lists Renaissance women Christine de Pizan and Teresa of Avila, several non-Western classics (*The Analects* of Confucius, *The Way of Lao Tsu*, the *Bhagavad Gita*, *The Teachings of the Compassionate Buddha*), Virginia Woolf, and Ralph Ellison. Shimer College now includes works by Woolf, Martin Luther King, Carol Gilligan, Frantz Fanon, and Michel Foucault, and notes in its admissions literature that "new works are judiciously added to those forming the core curriculum, particularly in light of those voices originally overlooked in the formation of the canon."[4] Favorites at other schools, besides those mentioned so far, are *The Epic of Gilgamesh*, Mary Wollstonecraft, Mary Shelley, and Toni Morrison.

Nontraditional listings like these occupy only a small portion of most great books programs, although Saint Mary's College (California), in a move that goes beyond what many reform canonists would support, has added to its four-course great books sequence (which already contains works by Wollstonecraft, Woolf, King, Morrison, Garcia Marquez, and several others outside of mainstream lists) an optional fifth course devoted entirely to the writings of four nontraditional groups: Native American, African American, Chicano/Latino, and Asian American. Also beyond the pale for many reformists is the step taken by the W. W. Norton and Company, publisher of widely used literature anthologies, to issue separately bound collections of writings by female authors and black authors, the existence of which is sometimes interpreted as bestowing quasi- or alternative canonical status. More in keeping with reformist thinking are Norton's *Anthology of American Literature*, which for many years has included significant (at least 20 percent) authorship by women and minorities, and the *Anthology of World Literature*, which originally covered only Western works, but now has non-Western ones as well.

Reform canonists who make additions such as these to the curriculum differ with their more strict colleagues on several counts. Reformists are more willing to give consideration to the results women's studies, black studies, and other nontraditional fields have produced by dredging for historically forgotten works. The reform position says that such works are deserving of reassessment and, as a result, a few will find places in the canon. Works should not be added, it is emphasized, *because* they are by females or minorities, but that status, which implies past prejudice, is an accepted reason for giving them a new review. During the review they must stand on their own merits.

Regarding the inclusion of contemporary writings, those that have not yet existed long enough to have stood the test of time, the reform approach is cautious, but willing to take an occasional chance on predicting which ones will eventually make the grade. The point of including these works is that the purpose of reading the canon is to prepare students for life here and now. While the great books of the past speak in important ways to the present, there may be contemporary messages that have not been presented in past writings and that students should be exposed to. After all, it is fully expected that some works that are now contemporary will eventually survive the test of time, and well-trained intellectuals should be able to make reasonable guesses as to which ones. If those guesses turn out to have been wrong, students still will have been exposed to contemporary thinking.

The reform position on non-Western works rejects the argument that a great divide of languages and thinking prevents Western readers from comprehending writings outside of their own basic tradition. Good English translations are available that give us access to the ideas of non-Western authors, translations made by experts knowledgeable of both the West and non-West. And the practice of using translations has long been employed in teaching the Western canon. Most of the great books of our tradition were written in Greek, Latin, French, and German, among other languages, and are not read by American students today in the original. But what of the ideas that translations of non-Western works convey? Are they so foreign to us, as the strict canonist position says, that American students will be incapable of understanding them? Some Western works may be easier to connect with than non-Western ones, but not all. Reading Aristotle's *Metaphysics* or Kant's *Critique of Pure Reason*, for instance, is likely to produce more puzzlement than the *Bhagavad Gita* or the *Epic of Gilgamesh*. The struggle to comprehend non-Western works is not beyond the level we expect of students who tackle the Western canon.

Plurality and Canon Revision

Among the features of anticanonism explained in Part II, one need-ing further attention is the criticism of the authorship of the canon. Three concerns were noted: (1) certain groups of authors have been treated unjustly in the canonization process; (2) key ideas espoused by those authors are lacking in the canon; and (3) students fail to get a proper variety of authorial role models. The first complaint concen-trates on female and minority authors. It is sometimes heard also about non-Western authors, but their circumstance is actually quite different and it will be discussed separately.

In general terms the complaint is a sensible one. Although theorists like Tompkins go too far in their characterization of canon formation as mainly political, we should not go to the other extreme and think that politics have been absent from the process. We cannot deny that, historically, females and minorities have lacked opportunity compared with that of white males. Clearly they were subjected to prejudices that reduced their chances for canonization. Common lore, as well as the writings of prominent intellectuals and canonical authors, long held that women and blacks have lesser capacity for intellectual accomplishment than white males. We have been reminded by black studies and women's studies scholars that the likes of Bacon, Hume, Kant, and Hegel made disparaging comments about the intellect of blacks, and that Thomas Jefferson condescendingly panned the poetry of former slave Phyllis Wheat-ley.[5] Hawthorne is now known not only for the books he wrote, but also for his comment about the "damned mob of scribbling women," and even prominent female writers have themselves expressed reser-vations about the quality of writing by their own sex. George Eliot, for instance, penned a witty essay entitled "Silly Novels by Lady Novelists," and Willa Cather is known to have remarked that "when I see the announcement of a new book by a woman, I—well I take one by a man instead."[6]

Sentiments like these did not keep all female and minority authors down, and some of them achieved canonical status. But what should we do about the possibility that others wrote works of excellence that suffered from tainted images and failed to make it through the canonization process? Rather than accept, as strict canonists suggest, that history's pronouncements cannot be changed, it is possible to look back at the past and recall some of it that has been obscured. We cannot change the fact that female and minority writings had relatively little impact on history, but we can ask if there are works of excellence that should be reconsidered for possible canonization. If there are some of truly great quality, we can have the benefit of reading them in the future. While they have not met the test of being revered across time, their quality can be reexamined by contemporary tribunal to determine if belated reverence is warranted.

To understand the situation better, consider an analogy with baseball. The Baseball Hall of Fame is a collection of greats in its field of human endeavor. There are annual reviews of retired players, and tough standards mean that only a very few are selected. Usually, selection occurs within a certain number of years after a player's retirement, or that player is destined to obscurity. However, the controllers of the Hall have a "Veterans" category that ensures that long-dead and forgotten players will still have a chance for consideration. In recent years, historians have recalled that earlier in the century there were professional "negro" leagues that played high-caliber baseball; occasionally their teams played against white major-league teams, and when they did they competed quite successfully. Social prejudices may have caused these teams to be forgotten, but when their players' accomplishments are recalled and put into fair perspective, a few greats are found. They are being nominated and voted into the Hall of Fame. The nomination process takes past prejudice into account, but nominees are elected only if their credentials indicate excellence as judged by the general standards to which all nominees are subjected.

Dealing with past injustices in canon formation can take a tip from baseball. The sensible answer is to extend equal opportunity now to those who were previously denied it. To do so requires the affirmative action measure of searching out those who have produced forgotten but excellent works. This is affirmative action in its original meaning: giving a boost in the search process by getting nontraditional candidates into the candidate pool. It is not the newer meaning of affirmative action that says nontraditional candidates must be selected or that the candidate pool will be restricted to only nontraditional candidates. The newer meaning sacrifices quality of performance for equality of social representation. The proper approach to adding past female and minority authors to the canon takes their marginalized status into account when adding them to the candidate pool, but then requires that they meet the same standards of excellence as their traditional counterparts.

What should the expected outcome be of re-reviews of past female and minority authors? Elizabeth Fox-Genovese, who is a strong supporter of teaching the canon and, at the same time, a leading figure in women's studies, has noted about writings by women,

> The past two decades of scholarship in feminism have vastly enriched our knowledge of women's writings in particular, and intellectual and cultural work in general. They have not recovered some lost female Shakespeare.[7]

Fox-Genovese celebrates the effect that reexamining women's writings has had on the literary establishment, but she does not rush to pack the canon with female authors who enter on a special credential of gender. She signals a gradual and careful approach whereby female-authored writings that are not unknown but still have been largely neglected by posterity are now given new consideration in light of contemporary social concerns. For instance, Mary Wollstonecraft's *A Vindication of the Rights of Woman* (late eighteenth century) and Virginia Woolf's *A Room of One's Own* and *To The Lighthouse* (early twentieth century) were not unknown to earlier critics, but they had not been given high marks by enough of them to be placed on great books lists. In recent years they have begun to appear on those lists.

The recent attention given to authors like Wollstonecraft and Woolf demonstrates that canon revision can occur and is occurring, although it takes time and requires deliberation and debate by many people. Such authors are still far from being universally accepted as having written great works, but they are reaching the threshold of canonization. Social pressure to give equal opportunity to women has led to reconsidering their literary significance, but their works are having to withstand the scrutiny of harsh critics. It is coming to be recognized that they speak in a potent fashion about ideas that have a resounding effect today.

It is what the reassessed works have to say, not who wrote them, that should lead to their canonization. But given that this is the case, and that female authors are thus accorded belated equal treatment with men, it is reasonable to assume that the number of canonized female authors from the past will remain small. One reason for this is the historical fact agreed upon by canonists (strict and reform) and anticanonists alike that, until relatively recently, far fewer women than men were authors. Eventually, scholars will exhaust the pool of names for reconsideration, and from that limited pool only a few works can be expected to bear the mark of greatness. The other reason for a continued dearth of female authors from the past, a reason that could also carry over to authors from the present and future, is the tendency for women's writings to be identified predominantly with social protest against sexism. This topic is of much concern in contemporary life, and it is leading to the belated canonization of authors like Wollstonecraft who wrote about women's lot before it was considered fashionable to do so. However, there is a danger that female authors are being pigeonholed as writing important works on this topic but not on others. Their access to canonization could thus become limited to the portion of the canon dealing with this topic. The great books address numerous topics, of which the condition of women is but one.

Much of the responsibility for identifying great female authorship with the writing of protest literature goes to women's studies scholars and boosters. They often ignore women's writings that do not fit in with a preconceived feminist attitude. While this exclusionary approach is followed unconsciously in some instances, at times it is consciously and purposely injected into the process of canon formation. It is clearly evident in the content of many anthologies of women's writings, and is stated boldly and summarily in the introduction to *The Feminist Companion to Literature in English*, which says that in determining what entries were to be included within its pages the editors gave preference

> to women whose works reflect awareness of their condition as women and as writers. (Few indeed are works by women which do not do this: those of our writers who are not in some sense feminists are mostly anti-feminists). We have shaped the entries to catch and transmit the signals of this awareness.[8]

While the shaping suggested here would disregard female authors who fail to deal with women's protest concerns, many canon-makers coming from this perspective still envision their type of revision as potentially pervasive rather than limited. Instead of conceiving of women's concerns as a topic, as one of many and thus entitled only to a small amount of shelf space, they see it in terms of the "female perspective" or point of view. That is, it is an entire way of thinking; it is not just what women write about, but how they see the world and life per se, that sets them apart from men. An extreme version of this thesis claims the "female perspective" applies in all subjects that people think and write about, and the claim is consistent with the anticanonist notion, lying in the background, that context is all-consuming, the context in this case being the femaleness of an author.

The problem with elevating the "female perspective" in this way is that it seems to apply to only some female-authored writings. It does not seem to be genderwide: some women do not espouse it at all, and others do so only when they are writing on certain subjects. Further, it is sometimes espoused by men who have taken up the cause of women's concerns. The "female perspective," then, to the extent that it can be identified as such, is, as some critics have labeled it, *feminist* rather than *feminine*. Taking the form of an *ism* it might be as broad as, say, socialism, or as restricted as the Marxist version of socialism. But in either case it fails to take into account the writings of women that lie outside its purview. In the interest of dealing with historical prejudice against women as authors, and ensuring that it is not continued in the future, an effort should be made to give full and fair treatment to all female-authored works, not just those espousing a particular point of view. If feminist works are pushed into prominence out of proportion to their place among female-authored writings, their authors will have been given unfair and prejudicial advantage, and female authorship on the whole will be misrepresented and too narrowly conceived.

What has been said here about female authors holds in similar fashion for minority authors, with black authors as the prime example. They are absent from traditional great books lists, but it is possible for us to reassess their writings in light of equal opportunity and affirmative action. Presently, with a boost from the field of black studies, a few black authors from the nineteenth and twentieth centuries are being accorded the recognition that is moving them toward canonization. The writings of W. E. B. Du Bois and Ralph Ellison are good examples, comparable among their group to female authors like Wollstonecraft and Woolf. But as we look toward a time when such reassessment is completed, it should be expected that the number of canonized black authors will remain relatively small, given first of all that the practices of slavery and segregation limited access to quality education and the gateways of literary culture. However, there is also the factor of black authors being stereotyped. The collective message that those of growing reputation are taken to represent is protest against racism. While black authors have deepened our understanding of racism's harms, and its subtleties and persistence, it would be a great disservice if, as a whole, they became identified too strongly with the single theme of antiracism.

The preceding discussion about injustice to authors, and about misguided corrective measures to deal with it, does not transfer well to the case of non-Western authors. Anticanonists have sometimes lumped them together with Western women and minorities as victims of injustice by canon-makers, typically in general statements noting they are all missing from traditional reading lists. While it is true that non-Western authors are missing from those lists just as females and minorities are, and true that prejudicial assessments have sometimes surfaced against non-Western intellectual accomplishments just as they have against the accomplishments of females and minorities, the Western and non-Western "victims" differ from one another significantly.

First, it can be asked if leaving non-Western authors off Western reading lists is an injustice of the same sort or degree as leaving off authors native to the West; or, is it in fact an injustice at all? Non-Western authors have not been denied a chance for prominence—they have had that chance in their own cultures. And they have achieved prominence there. And the Western reaction to their works, while sometimes condescending, has often hailed them as great monuments that are as important in global terms as are the canonical works of the West. The *Bhagavad Gita*, *Upanishads*, *Koran*, and so on, even if not widely read in the West, have commanded respect in the West that has not been afforded to the writings of Western females and minorities. Western canon-makers have not left such non-Western works off their lists because of questions about their greatness; rather, it is because of their perceived differentness from Western thinking.

When efforts have been made to revise the canon by adding non-Western works, the limiting factors we noted concerning Western female- and minority-authored works have not appeared, or at least not to a significant extent. There is not a question of great non-Western works being mainly protest statements against political oppression. The great works of the non-Western world deal with many issues, just as do their counterparts in the West. And there is not a question of identifying a non-Western perspective or way of thinking analogous to those it has been argued are characteristic of important female and black Western authors. In all, claims of injustice to authors in canon formation, while a good argument for reassessing the writings of Western females and minorities, should be left aside when it comes to canon revision to include non-Western works.

Let us shift from discussion of justice to authors to the matter of authorial role models. The argument has been that if students see a canon comprised only or mostly of Western white male authors, they will come to think authors of other types are less capable, and thus the exclusionary process of the past will be perpetuated through psychological reinforcement. Here again a difference is evident between non-Western authors and Western female and minority authors, and they will be discussed separately, although there is a main point that applies to both.

Concern for students to have proper role models can hardly be disputed. But what can be disputed is the particular twist that concern takes regarding female and minority authors. If the corrective measure for their absence as authorial role models in the canon is, as many anticanonists have called for, to add or substitute female- and minority-authored works about sexism and racism, the image students will see is that important works by females and minorities are limited to those topics. This conclusion is based on the same line of reasoning as the original argument—that students will assume the capability of marginalized authors is reflected by what appears in the canon. It may be something of an improvement in image for female- and minority-authored protest works to appear there, but the gain would simultaneously seem to portray marginalized authors as of limited significance in the larger scheme of things.

Suppose, on the other hand, that the corrective measure for white male authorship of the canon is to add female- and minority-authored works of any type, not only or mainly protest works about sexism and racism. Assume, too, that because of our history of repressing female and minority intellectual and literary efforts, only a few older works will be found that are reassessed to meet canonical standards. Even if a substantial portion of twentieth-century additions by females and minorities are made, the overall percentage of works by marginalized authors in the canon will still be fairly small. In this scenario the image students will see again constitutes an improvement, but only a slight one. Marginalized authors will appear only slightly less marginalized than before in the larger scheme of things.

What psychological effect will the images these scenarios suggest have on today's students? The notion that they will thereby think of females and minorities as less capable of authorship than white males seems hyperbolic. What both scenarios rely upon is the assumption that students' views about authorial capability will be affected greatly by the images they absorb from a table of contents of authors. But the assumption should be tempered considerably by recognizing that students today are already aware, without specific reference to the canon, that sexism and racism are part of our history, and that measures have been taken to deal with these problems. What students are likely to think is that the makeup of the canon, including its revisions, reflects history accurately: they will see that when the opportunity for authorship was extended to females and minorities in the twentieth century, those groups responded quite capably. And they can be expected to continue to do so in the future.

Discussions of, and signals about, gender and race relations are prevalent in our society, evident in the workplace, on popular television shows, and in many school curricula. Students realize that women and minorities are entering various professional fields today from which they were largely restricted in the past (law, for instance). They recognize that the marginalized people entering these fields are capable, and are demonstrating it by being subjected to the same standards as white males. Female and minority attorneys do, after all, have to make their cases just as white male attorneys do. Students have enough sense to apply this generalized perspective to the particular matter of authorship, and they can see that the lack of past accomplishment by females and minorities does not mean a lack of capability. And even if they are confronted with the image of important female and minority-authored works being mostly about sexism and racism, again they should be able to generalize from the world around them and avoid being trapped by the image. To refer again to attorneys, they do not all specialize in civil rights law, although many of the more visible ones have. Students are not likely to draw from this image the conclusion that female and minority attorneys are not capable of pursuing other specialties. Nor are students likely to think that because the writings their curriculum exposes them to by females and minorities are mostly about sexism and racism, the capability of those groups is thus limited.

With non-Western authors there is not a question of creating a narrow image of them by adding their prominent works to the canon. And disparagement to their image created by absence from the canon has been balanced by respect for their greatness considered in international terms. To the extent that their image remains demeaned, the point applies here that was made about students today not assuming the absence of a particular group of authors from the canon means that group is not capable. Just as Western females and minorities are achieving recognition in our society far beyond what they had before recent times, so too with non-Westerners. The fashionability of equal opportunity has played a role in this phenomenon, as, we might suspect, have international economics and global shrinking due to advances in communication and travel. Non-Westerners now participate visibly and often in Western corporate dealings, teach in Western higher-education institutions, and form political groups and alliances to be reckoned with in Western countries. Today's college students are not unaware of this situation. They have grown up with it, and witnessed in their own lifetime much of the accelerating historical change it represents. They are capable of realizing that the absence of non-Western books on reading lists does not mean non-Western authors lack capability, but only that their capability had been given limited recognition in the past.

Of the three main concerns voiced by anticanonists about a lack of plurality in the canon, two have now been answered. Restricted access to the process of canonization that female and minority authors experienced in the past should be redressed, and can be and is, by searching out and re-reviewing their forgotten works. The concern about a lack of female, minority, and non-Western authorial role models turns out to be largely misguided: even if in a revised canon students encounter relatively few such authors, they will have adequate reason not to assume thereby that people other than Western white males lack authorial capability. The third concern remains, that the canon is lacking in key ideas espoused by marginalized authors. Here is where the case can be made most definitively for the reform canonist perspective on revising great books lists based on the principle of plurality. It is not who the authors are that is in question, but what they have to say. Male authors are sometimes included, if they present nontraditional thinking. Also, the inclusion of non-Western works, while of lesser significance regarding justice to authors and authorial role models, now figures prominently into the argument.

The traditional canon includes a wide diversity of ideas: it speaks to many issues and it addresses those issues from various and competing points of view. This point was made in Part II in rebuttal to the anticanonist claim that the canon is a bulwark of political conservativism. The canon is already pluralistic in its content. But the inclusion of nontraditional works can make it even more pluralistic. The forum of thinking to which readers are exposed can be strengthened by broadening it. The forum consists of the great ideas and various viewpoints available regarding each. If new ideas are found, or, what is more likely, new viewpoints are found pertaining to existing great ideas, the works embodying them should be considered for inclusion in the canon. The issues of race, class, and gender, about which there is so much interest today, are already dealt with in the canon, and treatments from left-wing perspectives are included, but there are still certain ways of thinking about these issues that are not represented and ought to be. That is why Wollstonecraft and Woolf, and Du Bois and Ellison, are now being included by reform canonists on their reading lists, along with more recent authors like Morrison and Martin Luther King. While Plato, the Bible, Mill, Marx, Dickens, Ibsen, and others from the traditional canon speak against the oppression of certain marginalized people, they do not go as far or as deeply into matters as various nontraditional authors do.

Even though Mill, for instance, in *The Subjection of Women*, made a case for the liberation of women, he nonetheless pictured the division of labor between the sexes as appropriately remaining separated between domesticity for women and the professions for men. Woolf's *A Room of One's Own* takes the case of liberation farther, exploring, among other things, how the web of domesticity can inhibit the development and fulfillment of personal and professional talents and urges. Ellison's *Invisible Man* picks up on Du Bois's perspective on double-consciousness, giving an extended demonstration of the "twoness" experienced by black people in their minds and in the world around them—being American and being black, living in the land of freedom but on a floating island of restriction. Other authors had decried the servitude of blacks first under slavery and then under segregation, but Ellison presents a trenchant examination of the psychological depths of racism. We see that as broad and pluralistic as the traditional canon is, it can be made more so by adding new voices on matters of race, class, and gender.

The desire to broaden the canon should stand as a given, a basic assumption, for canonists who see the purpose of studying the canon (or at least one of its purposes) to be the promotion of critical thinking. The time-honored argument that the canon should be studied because it expands students' minds by giving them rigorous mental exercise, especially by confronting them with powerful and competing thoughts on the most vital and difficult issues for the human mind, converts easily into an argument for revising the canon to include ways of thinking not included previously. The broader the base of the canon, the more students have to think about, the greater their mental stimulation, and the greater are the ways of thinking they can try on, analyze, criticize.

The pedagogical function of promoting critical thinking is thus enhanced by revising the canon. Students' minds are opened to new ways of thinking and they become practiced at dealing with complex issues by seeing various angles on them. The new perspectives on race, class, and gender are in this sense mechanisms to challenge the mind and sharpen it. They are like new strategies a chess player is confronted with by a nonconventional master. But these new perspectives also go beyond the arena of intellectual gamesmanship, beyond providing an occasion for students to hone the skills of their thinking processes. The issues of race, class, and gender are important in everyday life. The content provided by the new perspectives on these issues is important in determining what are the proper ways to live our lives, that is, what is the proper way to relate to other human beings. The essence of the reform canonist position is that students should be exposed to these new ways of thinking but weigh them carefully with the views of other canonical authors. The new views are not preached or covertly pressured upon students; nor are they denounced. They are simply added to an already existing corpus and afforded the equal status of being deserving of consideration. The new views blend into the much larger canonical whole as a part of the materials students will work with in figuring out their own answers to important questions about how they want to live.

Continuing the argument from plurality for expanding the canon is the prospect of including non-Western works. It is the differentness of such works that gives strict canonists pause, yet it is precisely that differentness that enhances the function of critical thinking by going beyond the range of viewpoints typical of our European-American heritage. When Adler and others cite great differences in Western and non-Western thought, what they often have in mind is the contrast between Judeo-Christian ideals and some of the basic tenets of the philosophical-religious systems of the Far East. Contrasted with the Judeo-Christian notion of God are Hindu theistic thinking, which has a different concept of deity; Buddhist thought, which (for many Buddhists) is godless; Confucianism, which embraces heaven, but with an ambiguous meaning to Western thinkers; and the Tao, according to which the reality of the universe is utterly impersonal, that is, has no personal relations with humans. In the Judeo-Christian view the world was created by God with a clear purpose and omnipotent will, with history being linear and goal-directed. Hinduism and Buddhism conceive of the world and history in cyclic terms, with no purpose and no real meaning, and an emphasis on reincarnation. Confucianism, Taoism, and Shinto thought see no meaningful eschatology that can tell of the ultimate destiny of the world and humanity.[9]

Differences like these are fundamental and profound, but not incomprehensible. Professional scholars and students who have specialized in Asian thought, as well as those who have merely dabbled in it, have benefited by having their horizons expanded, their critical perspectives enlarged, through confronting such differentness as it is found in the great works of the several Far Eastern traditions. The same opportunity should be extended to all students who read the Western canon for enhancing critical thinking.

But adding the classics of Far Eastern philosophy and religion to student reading lists does not constitute a complete answer to the prospect of internationalizing the canon. The contemporary emphasis on race, class, and gender brings to light ideas that come from outside of the Far East, and from outside our own dominant European tradition, that run counter to our political affairs. Native American culture, for instance, gives us the Iroquois Constitution, according to which women had a separate and powerful executive branch role in government. Voices from Africa are also heard, such as that of internationally acclaimed contemporary novelist Chinua

Achebe, whose works depict colonialism from the vantage of those who were colonized. Perspectives such as these add counterpoints and alternatives to the plurality of political thinking present in traditional canonical works, and their presence in the curriculum can thus contribute to critical thinking.

However, there are also qualifying factors to be kept in mind. Care should be exercised, in the interest of plurality, to distinguish for inclusion works that present truly different messages than are already present in the canon. Much of the postcolonial critique of Western culture has been based on the thinking of Marxism, psychoanalysis, existentialism, deconstructionism, and other Western movements. Postcolonialism in this regard is similar to European and American expressions of feminism and the protest thinking of minority authors. Trenchant extensions of Marxism, psychoanalysis, and so on, that offer new thinking about colonialism, as well as about feminism and American minority protest concerns, deserve consideration for inclusion on reading lists. Warmed-over versions of established perspectives do not.

Another factor to be kept in mind when adding contrapuntal political voices to the traditional canon is that some of those voices may be a far cry from, and in fact may be diametrically opposed to, the political preferences of anticolonialist, feminist, and minority protest thinking. If we are seeking differences from our own tradition, we should include on our reading lists, for example, works that place women in greater bondage than we do. That sort of difference is an eye-opener that should stimulate critical thinking. One obvious choice in that regard is the *Koran*. The role accorded to women (particularly through the institution of marriage) in the *Koran* is not in keeping with our European-American tradition. However, it is espoused by what is unquestionably a great book, not to mention being a practice of many people in the world today. Our European-American tradition contains within it a saga of developing liberality toward women, a branch of which eventually grew into contemporary feminism. Contemporary feminist concerns should be spoken for in the canon, in the interest of expanding plurality. So, too, should nontraditional views coming from the other direction. The prospect of internationalizing the political content of the canon to broaden it should not be conceived as loading up on its left wing.

A final point to be made concerning plurality and canon revision takes note of the anticanonist line of thought demanding that students read literature that allows them to identify with their own marginalized groups: black students with the "black tradition," and so on. Canon revision by the principles of reform canonism would allow for a bit of that identification, as black students would now find a small part of the canon speaking for their group, women for theirs, and so on. But the point behind extending the plurality of the canon for the purpose of critical thinking is to open students' eyes in many directions, not to focus them on one of the many lines of thinking found among great works. Plurality in this sense means looking all around to acquaint oneself with what is out there, not scanning, rejecting, waiting until something comes along that is different by way of identifying with the reader's personal political circumstance. Students who want to concentrate on writings of a certain type can do so outside of their study of the canon. The plurality of the great books exposes them to many identities, and in this way contributes to the development of their personal identities: they see themselves against different backgrounds. A revised canon does not lead them in the direction of being black or being female.

Cultural Unity and Canon Revision

Confronting the plurality of ideas found in the canon provokes students to expand their intellectual horizons. They think new thoughts and bounce them off old ones. Mental processes are exercised and strengthened, and the store of content to exercise them on is increased. Here is a good reason for studying the great books. But taken by itself the critical thinking argument gives pause to many canonist educators. The result of confronting a plurality of ideas may very well be confusion, resulting in a feeling of rootlessness. The popular term to describe this intellectual circumstance is "relativism," what some intellectual historians would identify as the essence of twentieth-century thought, and many canonists would cite as its bane. What do the many ideas to which students are exposed all add up to? What collective meaning can be drawn from, or lies in the background of, the critical-thinking process? Plurality needs to be balanced by a sense of unity. Relativism needs to be stabilized. Students need to develop a sense of who they are; they need to locate their expanding knowledge in a larger scheme of things. The larger scheme many canonists appeal to is Western culture. The canon, for all of its plurality, hangs together as a broad cultural tradition. It is this tradition that anticanonists want to break away from. Canonists, on the other hand, rely upon its presence.

The ancient Greeks and Romans recognized the importance of endowing their youth with an understanding of their own culture. Two of their main reasons were essentially the same as those echoed centuries later and summed up in William Bennett's dictum that we study Western culture because it is ours and because it is good.[10] Studying the roots of our culture tells us what we are by tracing where we have been. We can thus make sense of our customs and basic beliefs that otherwise would be vague or confusing when we confront them today. Pragmatically speaking, then, we can live our lives more effectively. And as we do so, we can accentuate the accomplishments that our tradition has achieved; we can celebrate them and ensure their continuance. Our tradition taken broadly as a whole provides a unity, a grounding that encompasses a variety of particulars and gives us stability and pride. The great books can be a primary vehicle for coming to know this unity, for learning about the framework upon which the culture we are living in is based.

At first glance, it might seem that the cultural unity argument for teaching the great books would support continuance of the traditional canon without revision. That is, it would seem that the unity within which the time-honored ideas and strands of European-American thinking are subsumed needs to be identified for what it is, rather than what revisionists would like it to be. The prospect of revisionism can easily strike fear into the hearts of supporters of the Western tradition that the canon represents. But if we give careful consideration to the rationale for passing on the tradition, we will find that the reasons of teaching it because it is ours and because it is good both support the prospect of adding nontraditional works to student reading lists. And to these reasons a third is added: whatever good is to be found in the tradition, there is still room for improvement. Knowing where our culture has come from and what it has become is an essential ingredient for identifying weaknesses in need of change. The judgments we make that tell us of our own failings require a sense of shared unity. As Richard Rorty has said about knowing the American tradition, a point that can also be extended to the larger Western culture from which the United States grew, "you can feel shame over your country's behavior only to the extent to which you feel it is *your* country."[11] We need a shared understanding of what our culture is, and *that* it is, before we can pass the judgment that it needs to be improved.

This third reason for passing on our tradition is appealing to many educators in the latter twentieth century who are sympathetic to left-wing politics yet are uncomfortable with anticanonism's brand of it and way of applying it to the curriculum. It was noted earlier that the anticanon curriculum employs the strategy of exposing students to traditional books and ideas as a negative backdrop for presenting preferred recent ideas about race, class, and gender. Where that strategy differs from the one Rorty speaks for here is in the amount of emphasis placed on political affairs as opposed to other matters when Western culture is presented to students, and in the degree to which there is recognition of the tradition as good as well as censurable. Anticanonism magnifies the significance of race, class, and gender, and accordingly finds the tradition strongly censurable.

The issues of race, class, and gender are not new, but are very much part of our history, our culture. And they have been written about in the past, although as we have noted, recent and rediscovered voices give us new perspectives. By adding those voices to student reading lists we can ensure that the picture students get from the canon about the unity we identify as the Western tradition is complete, comprehensive. When students read Du Bois and Ellison, Wollstonecraft and Woolf, they are not only encountering contrapuntal voices that galvanize them into thinking new and critical thoughts about certain features of the received tradition. They are in an important sense working within that tradition, finding out about parts of its makeup. It has always been a feature of the tradition that it generates internal opposition to itself. The oppositional voices are part and parcel of our culture. Even non-Western voices figure into the picture in places. Reading the *Koran*, for instance, helps us to learn about a significant element that has now entered Western culture, as many Muslims now live in the West and have carved out a niche here. So, when we add to our reading lists works dealing with race, class, and gender, and certain non-Western works, we are touching up the picture of our culture as it has been presented traditionally. We are enhancing it by making it fuller and more accurate. That is not to say that we should be doing a major job of repainting such that the traditional picture is unrecognizable. Its size and grandeur can remain intact while at the same time new elements are added or older but obscured ones are given more highlighting.

Still, while nontraditional works are found actually to be part of our tradition, there is no denying their "otherness." While works about race, class, and gender may be part of our culture, many of them also step beyond or outside of the tradition in the way that non-Western works do more obviously. Both allow us to look back at the tradition from an external vantage point as airplane or space satellite travelers do in viewing the earth: we resist the planet's gravitational pull enough to see things differently than we do when on its surface. This experience has the effect of helping us focus on particular aspects of our tradition for what they are, while also making them more understandable collectively, more recognizable as a whole. As Michael Oakeshott puts it regarding the particulars, "to investigate the concrete manner in which another people goes about the business of attending to its arrangements may reveal significant passages in our tradition which might otherwise remain hidden."[12] We dust off or uncover what might otherwise remain obscured. And at the same time the particulars are revealed to hang together in certain ways. The vantage point offered through nontraditional works puts our own tradition in relief and helps us to see just what the unity amidst its diversity consists of.

Further, beyond simply viewing our tradition in a unified picture, we are in a better position to come to judgments about it. As critics who have encountered "otherness," we are more capable of discerning our civilization's glory and its shame. The points of contrast with our culture that nontraditional works provide help us to see what is good about it and what is not. On the negative side, we are forced to confront the traditional roles women and minorities and the lower classes have been given in our culture. They have been more restricted than white males, disallowed or less easily allowed access to certain elements of life that lead to human fulfillment. To whatever extent our collective unconscious has forgotten or repressed or failed to incorporate this point, we are now very much aware of it. We are able to look back and say that there is a part of our tradition that in many of its manifestations we find objectionable.

In being self-critical of our tradition in this way we are following out still further that element of it that generates internal opposition. In this case the opposition constitutes more than the fact of interesting and significant oppositional voices that are part of the large picture. We come to an indictment of the large picture, about our past in general, about our views and treatment of women and minorities throughout our history. While such a generalization may seem risky, it follows a brand of thinking that some of our best-known philosophers have engaged in. Aristotle's *Metaphysics* begins with a critique of his predecessors, finding most of them far from his own preferred position. Descartes eschewed all previous knowledge in order to find a new starting point in the "cogito," from which he proceeded to build his own philosophical system. John Dewey is well known for promoting pragmatism by analyzing the errors of, and needed corrections to, the ideas of earlier philosophies from ancient Greece to the twentieth century. So the mindset that says we should get beyond our tradition to something that is superior to it is not a recent invention. In fact, that mindset is respected and repeated within the tradition, as some of the authors following it have been deemed great authors and some of their expressions of it have been incorporated into the canon. An important contributing factor to our culture's capacity today to be critical of our past on race, class, and gender is our historical willingness to listen to negative critiques of what we are about.

On the other hand, self-assessment of our culture should not be confined to figuring out what has been wrong with it and is in need of change for the better. When we step outside of the tradition and look back at it as a whole we should not fail to recognize its achievements. Our modern science, our philosophy, our industrial accomplishments are laudable, not only in self-congratulatory terms, but also in the view held by people from other cultures who have borrowed from us because they can see the superiority of what we have devised. That is, we should recognize what has been lacking in other cultures and is present in ours that makes ours advantageous. We have much that other cultures do not have but want, and this fact is a strong indicator of our worth.

And also in politics we have much to be proud of. While there are weaknesses, concerning race, class, and gender, an overview aided by stepping outside and looking back reveals not only those weaknesses, but also that it is in our own tradition that women, minorities, and the class-bound oppressed have made the strides that leave them today with a greater freedom and equality than their counterparts in other cultures now have or have had in the past. Where else have the principles of equal opportunity and affirmative action spoken as loudly as they do in the United States today, that is, in the standard operating principles of the quintessential heir of the Western tradition? Consider the foundation of our thinking about governance. Our tradition produced Locke's *Second Treatise on Civil Government*, the U.S. Declaration of Independence and Constitution, the French Declaration of the Rights of Man, J. S. Mill's *On Liberty*, and various other writings that provide the basis from which today's debates about race, class, and gender were able to emerge. While disparaged by anticanonist politics for being conservative (that is, racist, capitalist, and sexist), these are the documents that not only allow for our basic freedoms but encourage their further development.

Concern that the foundational political writings of our tradition failed to address aspects of freedom important to us today, and in fact continued certain assumptions antithetical to them, should not turn us away from the positive elements in those documents that are of overriding importance. If, for instance, there is regret or anger that women have been given short shrift in the tradition our basic political documents support, that stance should be balanced against the recognition that the lot of women in other traditions has been less free. The Islamic tradition, as spoken for in the Koran, is again a good example here, although other non-Western cultures might be cited as well. To whatever extent we may find our tradition to fail in its treatment of women, we should be open to the finding that other traditions fail more so. When we read the basic writings of those other traditions this point is driven home. Looking back at our own tradition in contrast with others should lead to a healthy respect for its strengths. Especially we should recognize among those strengths the emergence of political freedom.

Human Unity and Canon Revision

The cultural unity argument for studying the canon stands as a response to the concern that without such a sense of unity students will find themselves aimless and confused, possessors of much knowledge, but without being able to sort out what it all means. Some canonists are content to stop at the level of culture as the unifying factor behind the great books; they do not wish to think in terms of larger universals, and they are as suspicious as anticanonists are of the quest to locate a common human nature. They would speak as Rorty and Oakeshott do about the importance of our knowing and respecting the European-American tradition, but would back off from claims of a further sort of unity. However, other canonists see a need for unity at a level beyond the cultural. They, too, want to transcend relativism, but through a more comprehensive outlook than the confines of our own culture, however broad. When these canonists look toward the great ideas, they seek understandings common to humanity in general. This outlook is summarized well in a statement from a pamphlet issued by the great books program at the University of Notre Dame. A well-educated person

> is acquainted with and appreciates the best of the traditions of humankind, the values that these traditions enshrine, and the

principles upon which they rest. The intent of this wide reading is not cultural relativism, but a clear recognition of the universal values and the common problems of perennial interest to human beings.[13]

Why is it necessary to think in terms of such an all-inclusive unity? Why is cultural unity not enough, especially given the breadth and richness of the Western tradition? The answer begins by remembering that when we come to know our own culture we often want to take the further step of making judgments that require our extending beyond it and looking back at it. On the one hand, we make judgments about our culture relative to other cultures—we enjoy and revel in the high points of the Western tradition, and we congratulate ourselves as its product and preserver. In the same way we can note our culture's comparative weaknesses, its failures, and ask what can be done to improve it. On the other hand, we often make judgments that are not intended to contrast our culture with others, but simply to state a point of view, often a moral or political point of view, that we believe is true on a higher plane than that of our culture or any other. In both cases, the making of such judgments is part of the way we live. It demonstrates a tendency that is at least as far-reaching as the bounds of our culture, although the case might very well be made that the tendency is one of human nature.

In order to make judgments of such universality, we need standards by which they can be backed up. The standards need to be of a higher order than that of culture; otherwise we would not have escaped relativism, but rather would still be jeopardized by its far-reaching web. On what basis could we claim Western culture to be good or better relative to other cultures? If the answer is merely on the basis of Western cultural standards, it can be challenged as but one arrogant voice among other voices. On what basis could we claim a particular moral point of view to be the right one? If the answer is merely on the basis of the Western cultural tradition, or of one particular strand of thinking that appears in that tradition, again the challenge could be made that other voices have just as much authority.

Take the contemporary debate about race, class, and gender. It may be claimed that minorities, women, and those of lesser economic means are provided fairness in today's version of our cultural tradition, or it may be claimed that they are not and that further measures should be taken in the interest of justice. In either event, a standard above those at the cultural level needs to be invoked to support such a determination. Both sides, after all, are products of the tradition, tracing back to different strands within it. Without such a higher standard neither position can claim it is more in the right than the other.

Appeal to a common human core provides the higher standard that is needed. When there are competing claims about the worth of cultural traditions or of particular moral points of view, we tend to elevate our thinking to the level of humanity in general. It is a stronger claim to say one holds a view because it is in accord with what applies to the human species than that it holds because it accords with a lesser sort of unity. Thus appeals to redress the mistreatment of marginalized groups draw support from the assumption (often not stated directly) that those groups have been treated as less than fully human. Their basic human nature has been repressed, its fulfillment thwarted. The wrong or injustice that has been created lies in a failure to understand or respect that women, minorities, and people of the lower classes share with dominant white males certain basic elements of human nature from which their rights derive.

Human nature is perhaps the most obvious element in the makeup of a common human core. Certain moral judgments or points of view, including those about the politics of race, class, and gender, are seen to be supported by being in accord with what is natural for human beings; other judgments or points of view are seen to defy or distort what it means to be human. But there are differing and competing claims about what human nature truly consists of, and this circumstance leads to questions concerning religion, metaphysics and epistemology, and science. We think about whether humanity is related to a higher existence, and, if so, what the nature of that existence is and what type of relationship humans have with it. We consider whether humans can be observed typically to behave in certain ways under certain circumstances, and also ask about the appropriateness of the methods of observation. Further, we consider the nature of the physical environment in which humanity lives, and the circumstances it creates. Human unity extends to these matters in the sense that we assert answers that are meant to hold universally and thus carry the necessary force to support a moral point of view.

Still, there are differing points of view about these basic matters of religion, metaphysics, and epistemology, and the sciences, just as there are about human nature. This fact does not lead, as many people have thought, to the conclusion that there is no human unity but only relativism. Many of those same people, including contemporary anticanonists who propound a contextualist epistemology, still make claims they mean to hold beyond a relativistic framework, with many of their claims being about a morality that is assumed, if not directly stated, to be grounded in one view or another of human nature, which in turn may be grounded in a particular metapahysics, science, and so on. What those people are really saying or implying is that some views are the right ones and the rest are not, and that they know which are which.

In other words, what all parties making knowledge claims that they mean to hold universally rather than relatively must assume is a foundational unity. Even if there are disagreements about what it actually consists of, its existence is a given, a necessity. Study of the great books helps us in our efforts to figure out that unity's makeup. When readers wrestle with the great ideas the canon presents, they have the possibility of going beyond the critical-thinking exercise of pitting one view against another, and beyond the absorption of the collectivity of Western culture. They can, and quite naturally do, think in terms of reaching answers they hold to be correct, not because they bear the imprimatur of Western culture or some movement from within it, but because they believe they have consulted the relevant possibilities and weeded out the pretenders to come up with what is genuine. The key to the whole enterprise is having the possibilities available for consideration.

While the traditional canon is well equipped for this enterprise, it can still be improved upon by including readings from other cultures and nontraditional readings within Western culture. Readings from beyond the tradition, we have noted, help us to delineate the tradition more clearly, to see the outline and fullness of its unity. If we think in terms of a greater unity, again we find that traditional works do not offer all there is of importance that is available. In going beyond the tradition, we encounter thinking that stretches the boundaries of the great ideas, or universals, as the tradition has conceived them. Those fundamental categories may be the same ones the tradition has long recognized, but what are new are at least a few perspectives on them that now can be thrown into the arena to compete with those having established reputations.

To cite Woolf and Ellison again, the perspectives they provide push beyond the limits of traditional thinking about gender and race. Or, to apply Adler's categorical framework, we find that such great ideas as justice and equality are expanded.[14] When these authors and others point out the limitations on equality imposed through its psychological dimension and through socially deter-mined sex-role conformity, their approaches push us toward a more comprehensive understanding of what equality consists of than would be had through the traditional canon alone. They do not tell us all there is to know about equality, and the extent to which we should endorse what they do tell us is open to debate, but with their inclusion in our deliberations about equality we will at least try out new directions. Employing a metaphor that was introduced earlier, we will view an important intellectual landscape from new pathways while we also traverse the previously established ones, with the result that our overall grasp of the landscape is expanded. The landscape is a universal; it speaks to the nature of equality for human beings per se, not equality as it is seen in a particular context. Various readings from the canon, along with additions to the list, are all particulars that point from different directions toward an overall or inclusive unity we call equality.

Now consider the earlier example of the various conceptions of deity that are offered in great non-Western writings. Several concep-tions are available, all of which differ from that of the Judeo-Christian West. In studying these different conceptions we expand our horizons on a well-known universal. We go beyond the thinking presented in the canon, with the aim being to understand a universal in all its fullness. This fuller understanding allows us to talk intelligently about basic differences among cultures—we have gone beyond cultures to stand outside them and look back from a higher or more comprehensive vantage point. And this vantage point also provides the broad foundation needed for choosing and defending our choices of one conception of deity over another.

While canon revision in light of human unity can be supported by the reasoning offered here so far, there is still a challenge by strict canonism that remains to be dealt with. The point might be accepted by strict canonists that considering nontraditional Western works can expand our understanding of certain universals (although those same canonists might fall back on other reasons for not adding such works to their reading lists), but there is a looming concern about non-Western works. Other cultures are so different from ours, it is said, that making sense out of them is a task beyond our students and teachers. The fear, to borrow a famous quotation from Kipling that expresses it well, is that "East is East, and West is West, and never the twain shall meet."[15] The vision is of a great cultural divide that is unbridgeable.

One problem confronting many strict canonists holding this position is that they also accept the human unity argument as a reason for studying the great books. Through the great books, it is said, we can learn about universals of the human species and human knowledge. But in the search for such unity we should avoid other cultures because they are too different for us to learn from. Is there not an inconsistency here? How far can we go in searching for human unity if we refuse to consider cultures that we admit are different from ours yet are presumably part of the unity we seek? Human unity, after all, extends beyond cultural boundaries.

The anticanonist camp can be of some help in dealing with this problem, but it, too, ends up running aground on inconsistency. It points toward lessening Western fears about cultural differences, but balks at the prospect of universals. At least we are moved to ask such questions as: Are non-Western cultures so different from Western culture as has often been assumed? What sort of knowledge do we already have of non-Western cultures? Is there a way to cut through the "otherness" to a common ground beneath?

Edward Said, in his book *Orientalism*, now the primer for the rapidly expanding field of postcolonial studies, traces numerous instances in which the Western tradition has portrayed what it has called the "Orient" (originally, the term referred to the near and middle East, but has now been extended beyond) as different from the West, with that difference steeped in mysteriousness and thereby indicative of inferiority. Many canonical authors are cited, as well as lesser lights, who have portrayed the Orient in this way—Aeschylus, Euripides, Tasso, Cervantes, Shakespeare, Marlowe, Gibbon, Mandeville, Byron, Goethe, Scott, Flaubert, and Hugo, to mention only some.[16] With example heaped upon example, Said indicts the Western tradition for its arrogance and failure to understand what it finds different from itself.

But having pronounced his finding loudly, Said seems ambivalent as to what to do about it. He concludes the book with some vague yearnings about "promoting human community" and identifying with "human experience," yet in this book as well as in other writings he has stated strongly his preference for a contextualist approach to ways of knowing. He has spoken against the traditional canon of Western culture as politically homogeneous and repressive, yet he also holds that canons form an important part of Eastern cultures and admits that he has his own preferred books and authors (Derrida, Foucault, Gramsci, Benjamin, and so on).[17]

Said seems to sense the need for and possibility of pursuing human unity, and doing it through a canon of books, but his commitment to postmodern epistemology and politics gets in the way. He helps us to understand the way the West has often thought about the non-West, and he challenges us to reassess that way of thinking. But he puts aside the human unity thesis when it does not fit comfortably with other commitments he holds, even though it clearly invites further examination.

In spite of his inconsistency, we can learn from Said's commentary and many examples that, while the non-West is different from the West and has been portrayed as such, we can find evidence of human commonality when looking among various cultures. That is why students and teachers who have tackled non-Western works have found that they could make sense out of those works in spite of differences in culture. To refer again to Kipling's famous words, it should be pointed out that they were composed as the opening lines of a poem. But while what has been well remembered and popularized emphasizes the difference between East and West, the overall message of the poem is of unity.

> Oh, East is East and West is West, and never
>   the twain shall meet,
> Till Earth and Sky stand presently at God's
>   great Judgment Seat;
> But there is neither East nor West, border,
>   nor breed, nor birth,
> When two strong men stand face to face,
>   though they come from the ends of the earth![18]

The unity of West and non-West sometimes lies, as in the example of the idea of deity, in the fact that differences between cultures are subsumed by a common category. Differing perspectives on deity still deal with deity; human minds seem to be getting at the same issue. So what appears to be difference on the surface is still grounded in a common human core. But besides recognizing this circumstance, we should not overlook the commonalities among cultures that sometimes appear on or closer to the surface. Non-Western books can be found that say much the same thing as Western ones, thus providing not counterpoints to Western thinking on a given issue, but endorsement of it. The great ideas and the perspectives taken about them are reinforced as constituting a foundational human unity when we see that they come from other cultures as well as our own.

The key to getting beyond the popular lore of difference, and to moving in the direction of human unity, lies in recollecting the ties the history of Western culture acknowledges with the non-West. Both West and non-West have pursued the great ideas we are familiar with. We recall the medieval connection of Western Europe and Arabic culture in which Europe borrowed Arabic mathematics and science while Arabic scholars studied Greek philosophy. Scholars from both cultures were grappling with the same questions and issues, and going beyond their own cultural confines to do so. They recognized and pursued a common intellectual base.

The *Travels of Marco Polo*, written at the end of the medieval period, chronicles the strange and amazing sights its author saw on his journey through several non-Western cultures. Differences from the West are clearly evident and often emphasized, but elements of human unity still show through. We learn, for instance, that when Marco's brothers, who preceded him to China, met with the Great Khan, he questioned them about emperors, kings, princes, and other potentates. He then asked about their religion, and in hearing their explanation of Christianity, he charged them to request that the Pope send to him

> as many as an hundred persons of our Christian faith; intelligent men, acquainted with the Seven Arts, well qualified to enter into controversy, and able clearly to prove by force of argument to idolators and other kinds of folk, that the Law of Christ was best.[19]

In other words, the Khan wanted to discuss politics and religion, recognizing that for all of his differences with Western ideas, there were common questions and issues to be explored.

In the centuries that followed there were at least occasional instances where non-Western writings and ideas were known about and taken seriously in the West. *Tales from the Thousand and One Nights* was first published in English in the eighteenth century, presenting stories of genies and sultans and medieval life in the Orient. On the surface such examples are the stuff of cultural difference. But the collection of tales ranges from Persian to Muslim to Egyptian to Indian in origins, moving, then, across more than one non-Western culture, and in this way suggesting human commonality. And when we look beyond the genies and sultans to what the stories tell us about human thoughts and emotions and the vicissitudes of life, we find material that Westerners can share with the multiple non-Western cultures represented in the collection. We learn of love, hate, and greed, of startling awakenings of moral knowledge and reversals of fortune, of bureaucratic corruption and excessive mourning, of human successes and triumphs. This is the stuff not simply of one culture, but of all of humanity.

Early in the same century, the French author Fenelon constructed a discussion between Socrates and Confucius, clearly suggesting that West and non-West have something important in common to talk about. Confucianism has, in fact, often been referred to as paralleling the idea of Western thinkers who have asserted the natural goodness of humanity (Rousseau, for instance). And the image of placing Western and non-Western intellectual figures together is found in other instances of our cultural history as well, such as Raphael's fresco "The School of Athens," where Averroes is pictured together with Socrates and Plato.

In the nineteenth century the availability of non-Western works in the West, and particularly in English translation, grew considerably. The *Rubaiyat* by Omar Khayyam (written in the twelfth century) entered English literature, inviting cross-cultural commentary. Early on the poem was compared to a volume of poetry by A. E. Housman, and critic Charles Eliot Norton acclaimed it as speaking for his own generation.[20] The *Bhagavad Gita* was translated into English in 1785, and was read by curious nineteenth- and twentieth-century readers. They found notable parallels with Western thought, for instance, with Saint Terese on meditation, with Homer on work, and with Plato on reincarnation. Also in the nineteenth century the *Epic of Gilgamesh* was unearthed (originally collated by Ashurbanapal in ancient Assyria), which, when translated, was found to tell of such universally human themes as disaster resulting from hubris, a hero looking for fame, the revolt of mortal humanity against death, and savage versus civilization.

The examples could go on, but these few should make the point that we can read the works of other cultures and make sense of them because they deal with the same fundamental concerns, that is, the same great ideas, that the Western canon does. This does not mean that the perspectives they take are the same as those of the Western tradition—sometimes they may be and sometimes not. When they are, they reinforce what the canon tells us so we know that we are on the right track in the quest for human unity; when the perspectives are not the same they push out the boundaries of the canon's great ideas, helping us to see age-old concerns more fully.

Summary of Part III

Strict canonism rejects anticanonism, and also resists the proposals for revision made by reform canonists. The practical reason cited is lack of time in the curriculum for nontraditional works (time for the canon is too limited as is). But out of principle there is a rejection of the female- and minority-authored works that are presently receiving much attention. They have not met the test of time and are suspected to derive their popularity from trendy social protest thinking and sympathy for marginalized authors, rather than from a substance of greatness. Non-Western works are rejected because of language-barrier difficulties and because the ideas they convey are so different from Western ones that they will not be understood.

Reform canonism rejects anticanon extremes, but suggests that because prejudice has existed against the quality of female- and minority-authored writings (to a lesser extent than claimed by anticanonists), their works should be subject to re-review. Factors limiting the number of works likely to be canonized in this way are the dearth historically of female and minority authors, and the perception (encouraged by feminists and minority-studies scholars) that their important writings are limited to the topics of sexism and racism. Neither the same concern about prejudice nor the same factors limiting redress applies to non-Western works. Many such works have been acknowledged by Westerners to be great, and on many topics. The argument that students need to see female, minority, and non-Western authors as role models should be largely disregarded. Students today have ample reason to understand that the prejudice of the past does not mean that marginalized groups are lacking in authorial capability.

Reformists demand that canon revision be based on the content of the works that are added. The case is made to rest on the three main arguments typically cited for studying the great books: plurality (of ideas to promote critical thinking), cultural unity, and human unity.

The aim of fostering critical thinking is best accomplished by exposing students to as wide a range as possible of viewpoints on the great ideas; works presenting feminist and minority protest themes, as well as works presenting non-Western thinking, should be included so as to expand the range the traditional canon offers. However, when adding nontraditional works to widen pluralism, care should be taken not to focus only on the favored views of the political left.

Pluralism by itself can leave students confused and directionless. A sense of unity is also needed, and it is provided by the framework of Western culture, which we study because it is ours, it is good, and it is still open for improvement. The canon contributes much to this enterprise, but could contribute even more by being revised. Oppositional voices have always been part of our culture, and feminist and minority protest writings should be recognized in this sense as being part of our cultural unity. But in another sense they stand outside our tradition, as do non-Western works. From the exterior vantage point offered by both we can see better what the tradition as a whole consists of, which elements we should be proud of, and which elements should be changed.

Many canonists posit human unity as a higher sort of unity than cultural. It functions to provide standards by which cultural traditions can be assessed relative to one another, and competing points of view (including moral or political ones) within our culture can be judged right or wrong. Human unity includes the universals or great ideas associated with human nature, as well as others of religion, metaphysics and epistemology, and science. The great books are a prime means for coming to know the great ideas, but their potential can be improved by adding nontraditional writings: new perspectives on the ideas are thus provided, their boundaries stretched. Non-Western works are important here. The strict canonist fear concerning language differences is answered easily by the availability of good translations. The claim that the books are too different to understand is ill-conceived. It is inconsistent with the specieswide orientation of human unity, and with the fact that those Westerners who have tackled non-Western works have comprehended them well enough both to note similarities with the Western canon and to be awakened to new thoughts.

Conclusion

✿

SOME FURTHER THOUGHTS ABOUT CANON REVISION

THE PROSPECT OF CANON REVISION is supported by both history and sound pedagogical philosophy. One of the important points made in Part I is that the canon's contents have been subject to revision before. Revamping reading lists is not a new idea or unprecedented practice: it occurred in the past at key junctures when Roman works were added to Greek, modern-language works were added to classical-language writings, and the social sciences were added to the humanities and natural sciences. Part III presented reasons why revision is needed again at our present point in history. The addition of nontraditional works on race, class, and gender, and of non-Western works, will enlarge students' opportunity to develop critical thinking, round out their understanding of our Western cultural heritage, and move them closer to an understanding of the unity shared among human beings.

With all of that in mind, an important question remains that has been addressed partially but that warrants further discussion. Given that the canon needs revision, just how much of it should there be? It is one thing to recognize that a change is needed, but another thing to determine the proper scope for it. Canonists who are comfortable with the reform perspective may still be asking, "What are we talking about here—five percent of the reading list? Twenty-five percent? More?"

To talk in percentages sounds crude, and it invites the sorts of criticism usually made against quota systems, but it will be difficult for someone supportive of the canon not to think at least in less precise terms about establishing limits for the revision of its contents. If a numerical answer to the question is difficult or inappropriate, it is still possible to deliberate about key factors involved in setting limits, that is, to recognize the principles upon which limitation is to be based.

Of the three main arguments that have been discussed favoring canon revision, the critical-thinking argument would seem to leave open the matter of how much revision is called for. The objective of expanding critical thinking points toward adding great works that go beyond the received Western tradition, but that objective in itself presents no inherent reason for setting limits to the additions. The presumed outcome would be expanding human knowledge to its maximum, however much change that might require in the canon. Whatever number of new great ideas could be found, or new angles on old ideas, would be fair game.

The human unity argument, too, offers little by way of a principle for setting limits to canon revision. The broad boundaries of human unity, defined as common human nature and knowledge, would seem initially to embrace the same territory critical thinking does, with the difference being that human unity suggests working from that point toward identifying certain ideas and values of priority. That is, the pedagogical starting point to lead students in the direction of identifying human unity lies in the comparison and contrast that can be found in thinking through the widest possible range of ideas. The canon functions to provide that starting point and thus would be expected to carry across the full expanse of knowledge humans have achieved.

While critical thinking and human unity do not suggest limitations on canon revision, there are two important factors that do. One is cultural unity; the other is the breadth and shape of the overall terrain the human intellect deals with, and the degree to which the traditional canon already covers that terrain. Respect for the unity of our traditional Western culture stands as a powerful caution against overzealous canon revision. But perhaps even more important is the fact that in the grand intellectual scheme of things the traditional canon is already quite comprehensive. The combination of contemporary thinking about race, class, and gender and new insights available to us by consulting non-Western thinking, significant as it is, seems small in comparison with the expanse of knowledge the Western tradition has long offered.

Studying the canon, according to the cultural unity argument, prepares students to live their lives successfully in the cultural milieu by which they are surrounded. Giving them an overall picture of traditional Western culture generates pride and stability that can fend off relativism and confusion that might otherwise result. Also, students get a clearer view of weaknesses in the tradition that are in need of change. Revising the canon to include nontraditional works clarifies and touches up the overall picture they have of their cultural milieu. But if works atypical to the tradition are added too generously, the original picture will become distorted and the objectives of pride and stability will suffer.

As important as race, class, and gender may seem in light of current concerns for social change, the politics of these issues comprise but part of a much larger cultural whole. To make works keying on these issues to constitute, say, half of the reading list, would be tantamount to claiming that these issues amount to half of what it is important to learn about our culture. Students would be invited to think about the Western tradition especially or mainly in terms of this restricted focus. They would spend much of their time taking it on and refining it, and practicing at viewing the world through it. Even if the readings contained a balance of various points of view, and students were not imbued with leftist ideology, they would be led to see the tradition in terms of certain of its most controversial aspects. To emphasize controversy leads easily to the judgment that the tradition is unsettled or in need of transformation. And to emphasize certain aspects of the tradition at the unavoidable expense of diminishing the significance of many other important aspects, or ignoring them, leaves students without benefit of the overall attainments the tradition has to offer. They miss out on acquiring much that is valuable in dealing with our complex and confusing world. Thus cultural unity suffers as pride gives way to uneasiness and and stability gives way to change, and the potential for developing a comprehensive wisdom gives way to an invitation for confusion. Students will have been readied for the cultural-unity objective of identifying areas in the tradition where change may be in order, but that objective will have been accomplished at the expense of seeing the tradition in a broader and brighter light befitting the wisdom of many of its aspects other than certain political ones.

In the interest of giving students a fair portrayal of the overall cultural milieu of the Western tradition, and encouraging pride and stability of the many laudable aspects thereof, the addition of race, class, and gender works to canonical lists should be limited to an extent where they do not rival or overcome the rest of the tradition. The addition of such works is important, and consistent with the pursuit of cultural unity, but it must be weighed in reasonably vis-à-vis the tradition as a whole.

Turning from a Western, and especially American, emphasis on race, class, and gender to the addition of non-Western works, we encounter a potentially broader and more complex challenge to the tradition. Non-Western works range far beyond those political matters, and they come from many national and ethnic groups that represent several major cultural traditions. It would be easy to conceive of non-Western works as assuming majority control of a revised canon, with substantial representation given to each major culture, and Western works left as a minority.

The canon could become truly internationalized in this way, but again the cultural-unity objective of stability would suffer. The emphasis would shift from preparing students for the Western world they inhabit to preparing them for the larger unity of a global culture. Such a global culture does not exist at present, although it can be argued that there is movement in that direction. Since we are far from being there yet, and it is merely conjecture to think we will be at some point in time, the objectives of cultural unity demand that our greatest attention still be placed on the Western ideas that are our own.

We can think back here to Adler's earlier-quoted words.

> In the distant future there may be a single worldwide cultural community with one set of common basic ideas and issues; but until that comes into existence, becoming a generally educated human being in the West involves understanding the basic ideas and issues that abound in the intellectual tradition to which one is heir either by the place of one's birth or by immigration to the West.[1]

Adler employs this point in arguing that we should avoid adding non-Western works to the canon. While that argument for avoidance has been rebutted, the point still speaks well as a principle of limitation. Non-Western works do belong on our reading lists, but the overall mix should be consistent with our present situation, which is predominantly Western. If too large a non-Western injection is made into the mix, then the collection of readings becomes an agent pushing for change toward a different cultural milieu more than a reflection of the reality of the cultural milieu in which we are living. Unity among cultures is a key factor to be considered in canon revision, but we should not lose sight of the foundation from which we look toward that presently unachieved sort of unity. To again speak metaphorically of the intellectual terrain, it could be said that we should look into the distance toward what is potentially the broadest, richest terrain, but to the extent that such a whole differs from our own part of it, we should approach it gradually while still recognizing the part which is ours.

The argument so far is that respect for cultural unity demands limitations on the amount of revision the canon should undergo to include nontraditional works. But, we may ask, by showing deference to cultural unity, are we underrepresenting the demands of critical thinking and human unity? Has one of the three main arguments for teaching the canon and revising it come into conflict with the other two and been given priority over them? If critical thinking and human unity call for a canon expanded to the widest possible proportions, why should the limitations called for by cultural unity be heeded? The matter of determining how one main pedagogical argument is to be weighed against the other two, if they come into conflict, presents a significant problem. The conflict may be mitigated, however, by considering just how much nontraditional works stand to add to the Western tradition so that the widest possible intellectual terrain is available for students to be exposed to. In other words, if we prescind from the notion that our own culture taken in its traditional form deserves priority, and we think in terms of human knowledge per se, just how much of that greater whole is not already spoken for by traditionally received Western culture? If what makes up the whole is for the most part already recognized by our tradition, then Western cultural unity is not greatly at odds with a curriculum that expands critical thinking and embraces human unity.

The notion of the whole of human knowledge here requires qualification. The reference is not to the totality of all things known to human beings, which might indeed find our own traditional culture outweighed by what lies outside of it. Differences among cultures abound concerning specialized knowledge—recipes for cooking, types and variations of actions performed in religious rituals, clothing styles and architectural styles and their subtleties, and so on. What is of import here is not such specialized knowledge, but what lies beneath it: the main or "great" ideas that are the building blocks for all human thought and for dealing with the major areas of concern in the way human beings live their lives.

It has been asserted, implied, and assumed at various points in this book that traditional Western culture does in fact provide coverage of most of humanity's great ideas, that race, class, and gender concerns constitute only a small amount of the collectivity of those ideas, and that non-Western knowledge adds only a limited amount to what Western thinking already knows of the whole. What allows for the making of such a grandiose claim? It does not issue from cultural hubris, but from taking an honest look at the intellectual richness of the Western tradition compared with what it has left out.

To appreciate that intellectual richness, it helps to consult a map of the basic ideas underlying Western culture. General encyclopedias could be useful, although they tend to blend specialized knowledge with knowledge of fundamental ideas, and they sometimes include both non-Western and Western knowledge such that it is unclear where the boundaries of the Western tradition are located. Standing alone in its thoroughness as a compilation of unalloyed fundamental ideas of the Western tradition is Mortimer Adler's *Syntopicon*, officially titled *The Great Ideas: A Syntopicon of Great Books of the Western World.*[2] Each of the 102 major ideas the book identifies is divided into its own topics (a half-dozen to a dozen topics per idea), most of which are, in turn, divided into subtopics. Justice, for instance, has eleven topics and twenty-eight subtopics, with some of the former being diverse conceptions of justice (with subtopics such as justice as harmony, as will or duty, as custom or moral sentiment), justice vis-à-vis love and friendship, justice and equality, justice and liberty (the theory of human rights), domestic justice, economic justice, and political justice (justice in government, with such subtopics as relation of the ruler and ruled, distribution of offices and suffrage, justice between states in matters of war and peace, justice tempered by clemency).

Another example is the idea of love. The *Syntopicon* delineates five topics and twenty subtopics. Within the topic of kinds of love are concupiscent, fraternal, romantic, and conjugal. The topic labeled "the social or political forces of love, sympathy, or friendship" includes love between equals and unequals, love and justice in relation to the common good, and the brotherhood of man and the world community. The other three topics comprise the nature of love, the morality of love, and Divine love.

It might be questioned whether Adler's 102 great ideas (see Appendix A for a full list) truly cover the entire intellectual base of our Western tradition. And the choice of what items constitute ideas as opposed to topics, and topics as opposed to subtopics, might be questioned as well, along with just how topics and subtopics are aligned relative to one another and within particular ideas. The map, in other words, may have its faults. But it gives us at least a rough picture of what the basic intellectual terrain of our culture looks like. It allows us to appreciate the tremendous scope of knowledge covered by the Western tradition.

We can expand the map to include previously uncharted territory represented by contemporary race, class, and gender concerns and knowledge available from non-Western cultures. But we will find that what they add does not compare in significance to what is already there to be added to. Many of the great ideas, topics, and subtopics have nothing to do with race, class, or gender. Some of them, of course, do, but most not to a great extent. Certainly those political concerns are pertinent to the idea of justice: they speak to such matters mentioned by Adler as equality, domestic justice, and economic justice. But as perusing the *Syntopicon* reminds us, justice involves many other concerns as well. Likewise with the idea of love: social and political concerns fit in, including those of race, class, and gender, but the idea itself is far more extensive than those concerns alone. Other ideas such as slavery, democracy, and family are obviously within the range the politics of race, class, and gender affects, but on examination, those ideas, too, are found to include much more. Ideas like punishment, will, and nature might be touched upon very slightly or peripherally, while dialectic, eternity, and time are outside of the range entirely.

The point here is that the totality of basic knowledge represented by the whole of the Western tradition is incomparably greater than that represented by race, class, and gender. It might be objected by anticanonists that the ideas, topics, and subtopics that are important change according to context, and that in our current context there are prominent political concerns that are more important than the features found on the traditional map. But such thinking would be equivalent to saying that if charting mountain ranges is currently in vogue among cartographers, the map of the world (or the Western world, if one wants exactness in the anology) should be redone so as to emphasize mountains. Other topographical features collectively represent much more than the totality of mountain ranges does. Even if it were maintained that past maps tended to leave out mountains or obscure them, and that greater emphasis on mountains is fitting, common sense still says that mountains are only one (even if important) feature in geography; the various other features to-gether count for much more. For all context can do to justify greater attention to certain political matters, it cannot alter the magnitude of the basic intellectual terrain that is out there to be seen if the mind's eye looks around at it.

While contemporary concerns about race, class, and gender are clearly visible to us, as is the map of traditional Western culture against which they are juxtaposed (if we care to consult it), non-Western thinking is more shadowy. We are aware of its existence and of some of its substance, but there is a tendency to conceive of it as vast territory, much of which has been uncharted by the West. How can it be said or assumed, then, that when the uncharted territory becomes charted it will not prove to be larger than what Western thought has identified? How can it be said that non-Western thought will merely supplement the traditional intellectual base our culture recognizes as its own?

The answer lies in the point made in Part III that contacts between Western culture and other cultures have revealed a good deal of commonality among them. There are many surface differ-ences that account for the obvious contrasts that can be drawn among cultures, but underlying the differences there seems to be a common human core. People from various cultures experience and think about justice, love, punishment, nature, and so on. And their contemplations get at many of the same topics and subtopics: the several basic justifications for punishment, the several sorts of love, and so on, are identified by people outside of Western culture and are written about in their books.

There are, of course, certain areas of thought—notably religion—where there are fundamental differences among cultures that should not be minimized. Differences of this sort should be charted on a global map of the basic intellectual structure that underlies humanity, and appropriate books should be added to ex-pand the reading lists of the West. But when that is done, we should ask honestly how many basic ideas, topics, and subtopics have been identified that are not already known to the Western tradition. There may be differences in emphasis to be accounted for in the relative weight certain perspectives on the same ideas are given by

different cultures; this is another significant factor not to be minimized. But, all told, when we ask what the West has not been aware
of, and that contact with other cultures has added to our understanding of the basic intellectual structure underlying humanity, the
answer is: not nearly as much as the Western tradition has already
known about.

While it may seem risky or unabashedly arrogant to make this
claim, its defense lies in the challenge to demonstrate that it is
inaccurate, that is, to delineate a collection of ideas that is different
from and overshadows the framework of the Western tradition.
Scholars who study the West and other cultures, and who are knowledgeable of the comprehensiveness of the Western great ideas, have
as yet not provided the evidence that would be needed to show such
difference, and many of those scholars would agree that an effort in
that direction would be futile. That is, they would recognize that
what allows them intellectual movement from one culture to another is a common framework of basic thinking shared cross-
culturally.

All of this is not to say that all cultures have been equally adept
at working out the great ideas underlying human thought and experience. The degree to which any culture has been can be determined
by asking the same question we have been asking about the Western
tradition: What does the culture's own map include, and what needs
to be added to it in order to complete coverage of the network and
cumulation of ideas that could be identified as global? Western
culture, to our best knowledge, has been highly successful at identifying and analyzing these ideas, and unless this circumstance is
disproved, we have good reason not to engage in canon revision in
major proportions.

In sum, regarding the demands of the critical-thinking and
cultural-unity arguments for revising the canon, it should be recognized that they press for as much revision as is needed to cover all
areas and perspectives of the intellectual basics available to human
thought that are not already covered in the Western canon. But
when it is then asked just how much revision that constitutes, the
answer is that, to the best of our knowledge, the great ideas offered
by the great books of Western thought cover most of the basic

intellectual terrain that other cultures taken collectively can provide, not to mention that the West may offer much that other cultures do not or are weak on. The canon revision called for by critical thinking and human unity, then, does not seem to be extensive. Students of the Western great books will be exposed through those books to most of humanity's views on the great ideas; the views they are not exposed to should be added through appropriate readings from other cultures.

Still, could it not be argued that while Western culture covers most of what students need to be exposed to, if a richly cross-cultural reading list were developed (with Western books not afforded a special emphasis), students could get the same sort of exposure? Western books dealing with justice, love, and so on could be replaced by non-Western ones that do the same. The advantage would be that recognition of human unity would be promoted. Students would get a forceful message that the great ideas truly do transcend cultures.

A detailed answer to this matter will not be attempted here, but must begin by going back again to the claims of cultural unity. Arguing from and for human unity is a respectable position; so is concern about cultural unity to be respected. To add to canonical reading lists a few works that duplicate the ideas of Western books on those lists, or replace the Western books, makes sense in the interest of pointing students toward an examination of the human unity that holds across cultures. But unless or until the world is much closer than it is now to a single common culture, it seems prudent for students within Western culture to be exposed mainly to Western works. Perhaps at a future time circumstances will have changed, but for now a reading list drawn mainly from the traditional canon of Western culture is still appropriate, supplemented by readings from outside the tradition that offer thinking missing from the tradition, and, in a few cases, that duplicate the tradition's thinking such that readers are led to examine and appreciate human intellectual commonality.

Appendix A

THE GREAT IDEAS

The list appeared originally in Mortimer Adler's *The Great Ideas: A Syntopicon of the Western World* (1952).

Angel
Animal
Aristocracy
Art
Astronomy
Beauty
Being
Cause
Chance
Change
Citizen
Constitution
Courage
Custom and Convention
Definition
Democracy
Desire
Dialectic
Duty
Education
Element
Emotion
Eternity
Evolution
Experience
Family
Fate
Form
God
Good and Evil
Government
Habit
Happiness
History
Honor
Hypothesis
Idea
Immortality
Induction
Infinity

Judgment

Justice

Knowledge

Labor

Language

Law

Liberty

Life and Death

Logic

Love

Man

Mathematics

Matter

Mechanics

Medicine

Memory and Imagination

Metaphysics

Mind

Monarchy

Nature

Necessity and Contingency

Oligarchy

One and Many

Opinion

Opposition

Philosophy

Physics

Pleasure and Pain

Poetry

Principle

Progress

Prophecy

Prudence

Punishment

Quality

Quantity

Reasoning

Relation

Religion

Revolution

Rhetoric

Same and Other

Science

Sense

Sign and Symbol

Sin

Slavery

Soul

Space

State

Temperance

Theology

Time

Truth

Tyranny

Universal and Particular

Vice and Virtue

War and Peace

Wealth

Will

Wisdom

World

Appendix B

✧

READING LISTS

ST. JOHN'S COLLEGE
Annapolis, Maryland and Santa Fe, New Mexico 1992–93

FRESHMAN YEAR

HOMER: *Iliad, Odyssey*

AESCHYLUS: *Agamemnon, Choephoroe, Eumenides, Prometheus Bound*

SOPHOCLES: *Oedipus Rex, Oedipus at Colonus, Antigone, Philoctetes*

THUCYDIDES: *Peloponnesian War*

EURIPIDES: *Hippolytus, Bacchae*

HERODOTUS: *Histories**

ARISTOPHANES: *Clouds*

PLATO: *Meno, Gorgias, Republic, Apology, Crito, Phaedo, Symposium, Parmenides, Theatetus, Sophist, Timaeus, Phaedrus*

ARISTOTLE: *Poetics, Physics,* Metaphysics,* Nichomachean Ethics,* On Generation and Corruption,* The Politics,* Parts of Animals,* Generation of Animals**

EUCLID: *Elements*

LUCRETIUS: *On the Nature of Things*

PLUTARCH: "Pericles," "Alcibiades," "Lycurgus," "Solon"

* indicates works read only in part

NICHOMACHUS: *Arithmetic**

LAVOISIER: *Elements of Chemistry**

ESSAYS BY: Archimedes, Torricelli, Pascal, Fahrenheit, Black, Avogadro, Cannizzaro

HARVEY: *Motion of the Heart and Blood*

SOPHOMORE YEAR

The Bible*

ARISTOTLE: *De Anima, On Interpretation,* Prior Analytics,* Categories**

APOLLONIUS: *Conics*

VIRGIL: *Aeneid*

PLUTARCH: *Lives**

EPICTETUS: *Discourses, Manual*

TACITUS: *Annals**

PTOLEMY: *Almagest**

PLOTINUS: *The Enneads**

AUGUSTINE: *Confessions*

ANSELM: *Proslogium*

AQUINAS: *Summa Theologica**

DANTE: *Divine Comedy*

CHAUCER: *Canterbury Tales**

DES PREZ: *Mass*

MACHIAVELLI: *The Prince, Discourses**

COPERNICUS: *On the Revolution of the Spheres**

LUTHER: *The Freedom of a Christian, Secular Authority, Commentary on Gallatians,* Sincere Admonition*

RABELAIS: *Gargantua**

PALESTRINA: *Missa Papae Marcelli*

MONTAIGNE: *Essays**

---

* indicates works read only in part

VIETE: "Introduction to the Analytical Art"

BACON: *Novum Organum**

SHAKESPEARE: *Richard II, Henry IV, The Tempest, As You Like It, Twelfth Night, Hamlet, Othello, Macbeth, King Lear, Sonnets**

POEMS BY: Marvell, Donne, and other sixteenth- and seventeenth-century poets

DESCARTES: *Rules for the Direction of Mind, Geometry**

PASCAL: *Generation of Conic Sections*

BACH: *St. Matthew Passion, Inventions*

HAYDN: Selected Works

MOZART: Selected Operas

BEETHOVEN: Selected Sonatas

SCHUBERT: Selected Songs

STRAVINSKY: *Symphony of Palms*

WEBERN: Selected Works

JUNIOR YEAR

CERVANTES: *Don Quixote*

GALILEO: *Two New Sciences**

HOBBES: *Leviathan**

DESCARTES: *Discourse on Method, Meditations, Rules for the Direction of the Mind,* The World**

MILTON: *Paradise Lost**

LA ROCHEFOUCAULD: *Maximes**

LA FONTAINE: *Fables**

PASCAL: *Pensées**

HUYGENS: *Treatise on Light,* On the Movement of Bodies by Impact*

SPINOZA: *Theologico-Political Treatise*

LOCKE: *Second Treatise on Civil Government*

---

* indicates works read only in part

RACINE: *Phaedra*

NEWTON: *Principia Mathematica**

KEPLER: *Epitome IV*

LEIBNITZ: *Monadology, Discourse on Metaphysics, What is Nature? Essay on Dynamics*

SWIFT: *Gulliver's Travels*

BERKELEY: *Principles of Human Knowledge*

HUME: *Treatise of Human Nature**

ROUSSEAU: *Social Contract, The Origin of Inequality*

ADAM SMITH: *Wealth of Nations**

KANT: *Critique of Pure Reason,* Fundamental Principles of Metaphysics of Morals, Critique of Judgment*

MOZART: *Don Giovanni*

JANE AUSTEN: *Pride and Prejudice, Emma*

HAMILTON, JAY AND MADISON: *The Federalist**

MELVILLE: *Billy Budd, Benito Cereno*

DEDEKIND: *Essay on the Theory of Numbers*

FIELDING: *Tom Jones*

TOCQUEVILLE: *Democracy in America**

ESSAYS BY: Young, Maxwell, S. Carnot, L. Carnot, Mayer, Kelvin, Taylor, Euler, D. Bernoulli

SENIOR YEAR

Articles of Confederation, "Declaration of Independence," *Constitution of the United States of America*, Supreme Court Opinions*

FREDERICK DOUGLASS: "The Constitution and Slavery," Selected Essays

MOLIÈRE: *The Misanthrope, Tartuffe*

GOETHE: *Faust**

MENDEL: *Experiments in Plant Hybridization*

* indicates works read only in part

DARWIN: *Origin of Species*

HEGEL: *Phenomenology,** *Logic* (from the Encyclopedia), *Philosophy of History**

LOBACHEVSKY: *Theory of Parallels**

TOCQUEVILLE: *Democracy in America**

LINCOLN: Selected Speeches

KIERKEGAARD: *Philosophical Fragments, Fear and Trembling*

WAGNER: *Tristan and Isolde*

MARX: *Capital,** *Political and Economic Manuscripts of 1844**

DOSTOEVSKI: *Brothers Karamazov*

TOLSTOY: *War and Peace*

MARK TWAIN: *The Adventures of Huckleberry Finn*

WILLIAM JAMES: *Psychology, Briefer Course*

NIETZSCHE: *Thus Spake Zarathustra,** *Beyond Good and Evil**

FREUD: *General Introduction to Psychoanalysis*

VALÉRY: Selected Poems

KAFKA: *The Metamorphosis, The Penal Colony*

EINSTEIN: Selected Papers

MILLIKAN: *The Electron**

CONRAD: *Heart of Darkness*

VIRGINIA WOOLF: *To the Lighthouse*

JOYCE: *The Dead*

FLANNERY O'CONNOR: *Everything that Rises Must Converge*

POEMS BY: Yeats, T. S. Eliot, Wallace Stevens, Baudelaire, Rimbaud, and others

ESSAYS BY: Faraday, Lorenz, J. J. Thomson, Whitehead, Minkowski, Rutherford, Einstein, Davisson, Bohr, Schrödinger, Maxwell, Bernard, Weismann, Millikan, de Broglie, Heisenberg, John Maynard Smith, Driesch, Boveri, Mendel, Teilhard de Chardin

---

* indicates works read only in part

STANFORD UNIVERSITY
Program in Cultures, Ideas, and Values
Philosophy Track
1990–91

AUTUMN

HOMER: *The Iliad*

Hebrew Bible and New Testament

THOMAS NAGEL: *What Does It All Mean?*

ANTHONY WESTON: *A Rulebook for Arguments*

PLATO: *The Republic*

Mencius

ARISTOTLE: *Generation of Animals*

MARYANNE CLINE HOROWITZ: "Aristotle and Woman"

NANCY TUANA: "The Weaker Seed: The Sexist Bias of Reproductive Theory"

W. E. H. STANNER: "The Dreaming"

ASHLEY MONTAGU: *Coming into Being among the Australian Aborigines*

ROBERT TONKINSON: "Semen Versus Spirit-Child in a Western Desert Culture"

CAROL DELANEY: "The Meaning of Paternity and the Virgin Birth Debate"

BRIAN EASLEA: *Fathering the Unthinkable: Masculinity, Scientists, and the Nuclear Arms Race*

PLATO: *Phaedo*

ARISTOTLE: *De Anima*

FREDERICK COPLESTON: *History of Medieval Philosophy*

ST. THOMAS AQUINAS: *Summa Theologica*

RENE DESCARTES: *Meditations*

WINTER

AUGUSTINE: *On the Free Choice of Will*

ERASMUS-LUTHER: *Discourse on Free Will*

SHAKESPEARE: *The Tempest*

KUHN: *The Copernican Revolution*

DESCARTES: *Meditations*

LOCKE: *Second Treatise on Civil Government*

ROUSSEAU: *The Social Contract*

EQUIANO: *Equiano's Travels*

FREDERICK DOUGLASS: *Narrative of the Life of Frederick Douglass*

HOGG: *Afro-American Slavery*

WOLLSTONECRAFT: *Vindication of the Rights of Woman*

HUME: *Dialogues Concerning Natural Religion*

GALILEO: *Dialogue Concerning the Two Chief World Systems*

NEWTON: *Newton's Philosophy of Nature: Selections from His Writings*

BACON: *The New Organon*

KELLER: *Reflections on Gender and Science*

FELDHAY: "Catholicism and the Emergence of Galilean Science"

NEEDHAM: "Science and Society in East and West"

SCHIEBINGER: *The Mind Has No Sex*

BLOM: *Descartes: His Moral Philosophy and Psychology*

AGONITO: *History of Ideas on Woman*

PIZAN: *The Book of the City of Ladies*

DE LA BARRE: *The Woman as Good as the Man*

HOBBES: *Leviathan*

JEFFERSON: *Life and Selected Writings*

THOMAS (ED.): *Slavery Attacked: The Abolitionist Crusade*

JACOBS: *Incidents in the Life of a Slave Girl*

RADIN: "Tlingit Trickster Myth"

RAMSEY: "Origin of Eternal Death"

C. H. HENNING: "Origin of the Confederacy of Five Nations"

TODD: "The Lost Sister of Wyoming"

FAIRBANKS: "Ethno-Archaelogy of the Florida Seminole"

PORTER: "Negroes and the Seminole War, 1835–1842"

SPRING

DARWIN: *The Darwin Reader*

MARX: *The Marx-Engels Reader*

FREUD: *The Freud Reader*

SIMONE DE BEAUVOIR: *The Second Sex*

KIERKEGAARD: "That Present Age"

J. N. FINDLAY: "Foreward"

FREDERICK DOUGLASS: *Narrative of the Life of Frederick Douglass*

HEGEL: "Lordship and Bondage"

JAGGAR: "Political Philosophies of Women's Liberation"

HARTMANN: "The Unhappy Marriage of Marxism and Feminism: Towards a More Progressive Union"

J. D'EMILIO AND ESTELLE FREEDMAN: *Intimate Matters: A History of Sexuality in America*

FOUCAULT: *The History of Sexuality*, vol. I

SMITH: *The Wealth of Nations*

GOULD: *The Mismeasure of Man*

PROCTER: *Racial Hygiene*

BALDWIN: "My Dungeon Shook: Letter to My Nephew on the One Hundredth Anniversary of the Emancipation"

HITLER: *Mein Kampf*

ARENDT: *Eichmann in Jerusalem*

BUTTERFIELD: *The Origins of Modern Science 1300–1800*

BERTRAND RUSSELL: "A Free Man's Worship"

WEISSKOPF: "The Origin of the Universe"

BORGES: "The Fearful Sphere of Pascal"

BERTRAND RUSSELL: *The Problems of Philosophy*

KANT: "Introduction to the Critique of Pure Reason"

KANT: *Prolegomena to Any Future Metaphysics*

BERTRAND RUSSELL: "Kant"

POPPER: *Conjectures and Refutations*

J. S. MILL: "That There Is, or May Be, a Science of Human Nature"

SKINNER: *Beyond Freedom and Dignity*

GEERTZ: *The Interpretation of Cultures*

PLAMENATZ: *Ideology*

LINDLEY: *Autonomy*

BALDWIN: "A Talk to Teachers"

WALKER: "Only Justice Can Stop a Curse"

LANGSTON HUGHES: "Harlem," "Freedom's Plow"

CHIEF SEATTLE: "Message"

ST. LAWRENCE UNIVERSITY
First-Year Program
Campbell College
1993–94

FALL

ANNIE DILLARD: *Pilgrim at Tinker Creek*

BLACK ELK: *Black Elk Speaks*

MAYA ANGELOU: *I Know Why the Caged Bird Sings*

TOBIAS WOLFF: *This Boy's Life*

MAXINE HONG KINGSTON: *Woman Warrior*

SEBRANECK, MEYER, AND KEMPER: *Writer's Inc.*

MIKE WINEGARDNER: "Elvis for Everyone"

KATHLEEN MULLEN SANDS: "American Indian Autobiography"

HIS HOLINESS THE DALAI LAMA: "Nobel Peace Prize Lecture," "Living Sanely"

PATRICIA HAMPL: "Memory and Imagination"

BELL HOOKS: "Writing Autobiography," "Talking Back," "Marginality as a Site of Resistance"

LUCY LIPPARD: "The Artist's Book Goes Public," "Conspicuous Consumption"

MAXINE HONG KINGSTON: excerpts from *China Men*

SPRING

JAMES CLIFFORD: "On Collecting Art and Cultures," *Out There*

LIZ STANLEY: "The Knowing Because Experiencing Subject," *Women's Studies International Forum*

BIDDY MARTIN: "Lesbian Identity and Autobiographical Difference(s)," *Lesbian and Gay Studies*

GLORIA STEINEM: "If Men Could Menstruate," *Outrageous Acts and Everyday Rebellions*

PEGGY MCINTOSH: "White Privilege, Male Privilege," *Race, Class and Gender: An Anthology*

HOMI K. BHABHA: "The Other Question," *Out There*

DWIGHT CONQUERGOOD: "Performing as a Moral Act," *Performance of Literature*

MICHAEL AGAR: *The Professional Stranger: An Informal Introduction to Ethnography*

JAMES FARIS: "Anthropological Transparency: Film, Representation, and Politics," *Film as Ethnography*

TIMOTHY ASCH: "The Ethics of Ethnographic Film-Making," *Film as Ethnography*

CATHERINE LUNTZ AND JANE L. COLLINS: *Reading National Geographic*

KAREN FINLEY: "We Keep Our Victims Ready," *Shock Treatment*

DAVID WOJNAROWICZ: "Being Queer in America," *High Risk*

DAVID TRINIDAD: "Eighteen to Twenty-One," *High Risk*

MALCOLM X: "Harlemite," *The Autobiographical Reader*

JAMES BALDWIN: "Stranger in the Village," *The Autobiographical Reader*

SANDRA CISNEROS: "Little Miracles, Kept Promises," *Woman Hollering Creek*

JOAN MORRISON AND ROBERT K. MORRISON: from *Witness*, "Two SNCC Interviews"

ELIZABETH BISHOP: "In the Waiting Room," *Geography III*

JOHN UPDIKE: "Men's Bodies, Men's Selves," *Harper's*

CHRISTOPHER BUCKLEY: "Time and Again," *Creative Nonfiction*

NOTES

Part I

1. Scholars have debated about the dates during which Homer lived, about whether he composed both or one or neither of the poems, and when they were put into written form. For the present purpose it is sufficient to date the *Iliad* and *Odyssey* approximately, and recognize that their immortalization, along with that of the name of their supposed author, begins the canonical tradition we have inherited.

2. This general-education aspect of the Sophists' program is sometimes overlooked in surveys of the history of education and the history of philosophy. More detailed analyses, however, include it. See, for instance, H. I. Marrou, *A History of Education in Antiquity* (New York: Mentor, 1964), chap. 5; Werner Jaeger, *Paideia: The Ideals of Greek Culture* (New York: Oxford University Press, 1939), vol. I, book I, chap. 3.

3. A recent and detailed account of the tension between the Oratorical and Platonic traditions, and how it continued through the centuries to the present day, is offered by Bruce A. Kimball, *Orators and Philosophers: A History of the Idea of Liberal Education* (New York: Teachers College Press, Columbia University, 1986).

4. Some of the lesser-knowns include Orpheus, Choerilus, Appolonius of Rhodes, Alcman, Alcarus, Callimachus, Epicharmus, Hellancius, Aristarchus, and Hipparchus. See Marrou, *A History of Education in Antiquity*, chaps. 7, 8.

5. Cicero, *Cicero on Oratory and Orators*, ed. and trans. J. S. Watson (London: Henry G. Bohn, 1855), p. 148.

6. Much of the collection was destroyed when Caesar besieged Alexandria in 48 B.C. The rest became ruins in 450 A.D. H. G. Good, *A History of Western Education* (New York: Macmillan, 1960), p. 84.

7. Quoted from Christopher Lucas, *Our Western Educational Heritage* (New York: Macmillan, 1972), p. 170.

149

8. Both quotations are taken from Helen Waddell, *The Wandering Scholars* (New York: Houghton Mifflin, 1927), p. xviii. The first is by Jerome, the second by Ermenrich of Ellwangen.

9. This list is drawn from David Knowles, *The Evolution of Medieval Thought* (New York: Random House, 1962), p. 74.

10. Good, *A History of Western Education*, p. 69.

11. A complete list of medieval universities and their founding dates can be found in Hilde de Ridder Symoens (ed.), *Universities in the Middle Ages* (New York: Cambridge University Press, 1992), pp. 62–64.

12. The Oxford list is cited in Lawrence A. Cremin, *American Education: The Colonial Experience 1607–1783* (New York: Harper and Row, 1970), pp. 197–98. Detailed information about the Oxford curriculum, and about other aspects of Oxford and other medieval universities, can be found in Hastings Rashdall, *The Universities of Europe in the Middle Ages*, 3 vol. (London: Oxford University Press, 1936).

13. Waddell, *The Wandering Scholars*, p. xxi.

14. Rabelais, *The Portable Rabelais: The Uninhibited Adventures of Gargantua and Pantagruel*, ed. Samuel Putnam (New York: Viking Press, Penguin edition, 1977), p. 265.

15. Jean LeRond D'Alembert, *Preliminary Discourse to the Encyclopedia of Diderot* (Indianapolis: Bobbs-Merrill, 1963), p. 65.

16. Jonathan Swift, "A Full and True Account of the Battel Between the Antient and Modern Books in St. James Library," in *Gulliver's Travels and Other Writings* (New York: Bantam Books, 1962), pp. 407, 406.

17. Ibid., p. 406.

18. Benjamin Franklin, "Proposals Relating to the Education of Youth in Pensilvanie, 1749," in *The Writings of Benjamin Franklin* (New York: Haskell House Publishers Ltd., 1970), vol. II, p. 394.

19. Cremin, *American Education*, pp. 382–83.

20. Quoted from Jeremiah Day and James L. Kingsley, "Report of the Yale Faculty," in *Foundations of Education in America: An Anthology of Major Thoughts and Significant Actions*, eds. James William Noll and Samuel P. Kelly (New York: Harper and Row, 1970), p. 204.

21. My summary of the introduction of English-language letters into the curriculum is drawn from Gerald Graff, *Professing Literature: An Institutional History* (Chicago: University of Chicago Press, 1987), chap. 3. Graff's book offers an excellent detailed account of the development of English studies in American higher education from the colonial period to the present.

22. The Great Books Foundation is based in Chicago and has been in operation for several decades. A list of readings for elementary and secondary students is available in a brochure entitled "The Junior Great Books Reading and Discussion Program."

23. Jacques Barzun, "Of What Use the Classics Today?" in his *Begin Here: The*

Forgotten Conditions of Teaching and Learning (Chicago: University of Chicago Press, 1991), p. 137.

24. William Bennett, *To Reclaim a Legacy* (Washington, D.C: National Endowment for the Humanities, 1984), p. 3.

25. Mortimer Adler (ed.), *The Great Ideas: A Syntopicon of the Western World* (Chicago: Encyclopedia Britannica, 1952).

26. William Bennett, "Why Western Civilization?" *National Forum* (Summer 1989), pp. 3–6.

Part II

1. Robert Scholes, for instance, discusses the canon as secular literature in *Textual Power* (New Haven: Yale University Press, 1985), chap. 1.

2. Roland Barthes, *Mythologies*, trans. A. Lavers (New York: Hill and Wang, 1972), p. 75.

3. Foucault interview in Ffons Elder (ed.), *Reflexive Water: The Basic Concerns of Mankind* (London: Souvenir Press, 1974).

4. This example is cited by Jane Tompkins in *Sensational Designs* (New York: Oxford University Press, 1985), p. 14. She takes it from Richard P. Adams, "Hawthorne's *Provincial Tales*," *New England Quarterly* 30 (March 1957), p. 50.

5. Stanley Fish, *Is There a Text in This Class?* (Cambridge: Harvard University Press, 1980), pp. 340–41, 348–49.

6. Barbara Herrnstein Smith, *Contingencies of Value* (Cambridge: Harvard University Press, 1988), p. 11.

7. Terry Eagleton, *Literary Theory* (Minneapolis: University of Minnesota Press, 1983), p. 202.

8. George Levine, et al., "Speaking for the Humanities," *Chronicle of Higher Education* (January 11, 1989), p. A16. This document appeared originally as American Council of Learned Societies Occasional Paper No. 7, 1989.

9. Stanley Fish, "Canon Busting: The Basic Issues," *National Forum* 69, no. 3 (Summer 1989), p. 13.

10. Elizabeth Greene, "Under Siege, Advocates of a More Diversified Curriculum Prepare for Continued Struggle in the Coming Year," *Chronicle of Higher Education* (September 12, 1988), p. A16.

11. Sheila Delany, "Up Against the Great Tradition," *The Politics of Literature*, p. 8.

12. Louis Kampf and Paul Lauter, "Introduction," in *The Politics of Literature*, p. 8.

13. Jane Tompkins, *Sensational Designs* (New York: Oxford University Press, 1985), pp. 4–5.

14. Alan C. Golding, "A History of American Poetry Anthologies," *Canons*, ed. Robert Von Halberg (Chicago: University of Chicago Press, 1983), pp. 283–84.

15. Sandra M. Gilbert and Susan Gubar, *The Norton Anthology of Literature by Women* (New York: W. W. Norton, 1985), p. xxx.

16. Sandra M. Gilbert and Susan Gubar, *The Madwoman in the Attic: The Woman Writer and the Nineteenth Century Literary Imagination* (New Haven: Yale University Press, 1979), p. xii.

17. Henry Louis Gates, Jr., *Loose Canons: Notes on the Culture Wars* (New York: Oxford University Press, 1992), pp. 65–66.

18. See especially Frantz Fanon, *The Wretched of the Earth* (New York: Grove Weidenfeld, 1963). Originally published in French by François Maspero, Paris, 1961.

19. Robert Scholes, "Aiming a Canon at the Curriculum," *Salmagundi* 72 (1986), p. 116.

20. Robert Scholes, Nancy R. Comley, and Gregory L. Ulmer, *Textbook: An Introduction to Literary Language* (New York: St. Martin's Press, 1988), p. v.

21. Steven M. Cohan, et al., "Not a Good Idea: The New Curriculum at Syracuse." Mimeo draft. I encountered this quote in Joel Weinsheimer's *Philosophical Hermeneutics and Literary Theory* (New Haven: Yale University Press, 1991), p. 125.

22. "Legislation for the Area One Requirement: Cultures, Ideas, and Values (CIV)," adopted by Faculty Senate of Stanford University, March 1988.

23. "Program in Cultures, Ideas, and Values: Required Readings 1990–91," Stanford University.

24. Gerald Graff, *Beyond the Culture Wars: How Teaching the Conflicts Can Revitalize American Education* (New York: W.W. Norton, 1992), and *Professing Literature*.

25. Graff, *Beyond the Culture Wars*, p. 31.

26. This quotation and list of books, along with those that follow, from the Saint Lawrence First-Year Program are drawn from the institution's course syllabi.

27. Hugo Meynell provides an excellent and fuller discussion of these examples and others in "Fish Fingered: Anatomy of a Deconstructionist," *Journal of Aesthetic Education* 23 (Summer 1989), pp. 5–15.

28. See above, p. 43.

29. See above, p. 43.

30. See above, p. 48.

31. Benjamin McArthur, "The War of the Great Books," *American Heritage* 40 (February 1989), p. 65.

32. Will Morrisey, "Ideology and Literary Studies: PMLA 1930–1990," *Academic Questions* (Winter 1992–93), p. 60.

33. For a more detailed discussion of Derrida's politics in relation to contextualism, see Thomas McCarthy, *Ideals and Illusions: On Reconstructionism and Deconstructionism in Contemporary Critical Theory* (Cambridge: MIT Press, 1991), chap. 4.

34. Jacques Derrida, "The Politics of Friendship," *Journal of Philosophy* 85 (1988), p. 641.

35. Gerald Graff, *Literature Against Itself* (Chicago: University of Chicago Press, 1979), p. 189.

36. Terry Eagleton, *Walter Benjamin or Towards a Revolutionary Criticism* (London: New Left Books, 1981), p. 112.

37. See, for instance, "That Old-Time Philosophy," *New Republic* (April 4, 1988) and "The Unpatriotic Academy," *New York Times* (February 13, 1994), p. E15.

38. Irving Howe, "The Value of the Canon," *New Republic* 18 (February 18, 1991).

Part III

1. Eva T. H. Brann, "The Canon Defended," *Philosophy and Literature* 17 (1993), p. 204.

2. Ibid; Leo Strauss, "What is Liberal Education?" *An Introduction to Political Philosophy: Ten Essays By Leo Strauss*, ed. Hilail Gildin (Detroit: Wayne State University Press, 1989); Barzun, *Begin Here*.

3. Mortimer J. Adler, *Reforming Education: The Opening of the American Mind* (New York: Macmillan, 1988), p. xxxiii.

4. The quote appears on a flier that is included in the college's packet of admissions literature.

5. A good brief summary of these and other slights is given by Gates in *Loose Canons*, pp. 57–62.

6. Quoted from Carol Iannone, "Feminism vs Literature," *Commentary* 50 (July 1988), p. 50.

7. Elizabeth Fox-Genovese, "The Feminist Challenge to the Canon," *National Forum* 69, no. 3 (Summer 1989), p. 33.

8. Virginia Blain, Patricia Clements, and Isobel Grundy, *The Feminist Companion to Literature in English* (New Haven: Yale University Press, 1990), p. ix.

9. For a concise summary of Far Eastern systems of thought, see Yong Choon Kim, *Oriental Thought: An Introduction to the Philosophical and Religious Thought of Asia* (Totowa, N.J: Rowman and Littlefield, 1973).

10. See above, p. 37.

11. Richard Rorty, "The Unpatriotic Academy."

12. Michael Oakeshott, *The Voice of Liberal Learning: Michael Oakeshott on Education* (New Haven: Yale University Press, 1989), p. 154.

13. The pamphlet is entitled "Program of Studies," from the Liberal Studies Program at the University of Notre Dame, Notre Dame, Indiana.

14. Equality is not one of the 102 great ideas around which Adler's *Syntopicon* is indexed. However, it is included in his later book *Six Great Ideas* (New York: Macmillan, 1981).

15. Rudyard Kipling, "The Ballad of East and West," *Rudyard Kipling's Verse: Definitive Edition* (Garden City, N.Y.: Doubleday, 1939), pp. 233, 236.

16. Edward Said, *Orientalism* (New York: Vintage, 1979). The book, taken as a whole, aims at making and supporting the claim that Western culture has portrayed the Orient as other, mysterious, and inferior. It is a detailed summary source concerning Western commentaries on the Orient.
17. A summary of Said's views on the canon can be found in Jan Gorak, *The Making of the Modern Canon: Genesis and Crisis of a Literary Idea* (London: Athlone, 1991), chap. 6.
18. Kipling, "The Ballad of East and West", p. 236.
19. Marco Polo, *The Travels of Marco Polo* (New York: Airmont Publishing Co., 1969), p. 16.
20. M. H. Abrams, et al. (eds.), *The Norton Anthology of English Literature* (New York: W. W. Norton, 1974), p. 1509.

Conclusion

1. See above, p. 86.
2. Adler, *The Great Ideas: A Syntopicon of the Western World*.

SELECTED BIBLIOGRAPHY

Adler, Mortimer, ed. *The Great Ideas: A Syntopicon of the Western World*. Chicago: Encyclopedia Britannica, 1952.

Adler, Mortimer J. *Reforming Education: The Opening of the American Mind*. New York: Macmillan, 1988.

Barzun, Jacques. *Begin Here: The Forgotten Conditions of Teaching and Learning*. Chicago: University of Chicago Press, 1991.

Bennett, William J. *To Reclaim a Legacy: A Report on the Humanities in Higher Education*. Washington, DC: National Endowment for the Humanities, 1984.

———. "Why Western Civilization?" *National Forum* 69 (Summer 1989): 3–6.

Blain, Virginia, Patricia Clements, and Isobel Grundy. *The Feminist Companion to Literature in English*. New Haven: Yale University Press, 1990.

Bloom, Allan. *The Closing of the American Mind: How Higher Education Has Failed Democracy and Impoverished the Souls of Today's Students*. New York: Simon and Schuster, 1987.

Bloom, Harold. *The Western Canon: The Book and School of the Ages*. New York: Harcourt Brace, 1994.

Bowen, James. *A History of Western Education: Civilization of Western Europe Sixth to Sixteenth Century*, 3 vols. New York: St. Martin's, 1975.

Brann, Eva T. H. "The Canon Defended." *Philosophy and Literature* 17 (1993): 193–218.

———. "Current Questions About the St. John's College Book List." St. John's College circular.

Bromwich, David. *Politics by Other Means: Higher Education and Group Thinking*. New Haven: Yale University Press, 1992.

Casement, William. "The Great Books and Politics." *Perspectives on Political Science* 20 (Summer 1991): 133–40.

———. "Unity, Diversity, and Leftist Support for the Canon." *Journal of Aesthetic Education* 27 (Fall 1993): 35–49.

Cheney, Lynne V. "Canons, Cultural Literacy, and the Core Curriculum." *National Forum* 69 (Summer 1989): 10–12.

———. *50 Hours: A Core Curriculum for College Students.* Washington, DC: National Endowment for the Humanities, 1989.

———. *Humanities in America: A Report to the President, the Congress, and the American People.* Washington, DC: National Endowment for the Humanities, 1988.

Churchill, John. "Great Books and the Teaching of Ethics." In *The Core and the Canon: A National Debate.* Edited by L. Robert Stevens, Julian Long, and G. L. Seligman. Denton, TX: University of North Texas Press, 1993, pp. 127–47.

Clausen, Christopher. "It Is Not Elitist to Place Major Literature at the Center of the English Curriculum." *Chronicle of Higher Education* (January 13, 1988).

———. "Moral Inversion and Critical Argument." *Georgia Review* (Spring 1988): 9–22.

Code, Lorraine. *What Can She Know? Feminist Theory and the Construction of Knowledge.* Ithaca, NY: Cornell University Press, 1986.

Craige, Betty Jean. "Curriculum Battles and Global Politics: Conflict of Paradigms." *National Forum* 69 (Summer 1989): 30–31.

———. "The Pursuit of Truth is Inherently Disruptive and Anti-Authoritarian." *Chronicle of Higher Education* (January 6, 1993).

———. *Reconnections: From Dualism to Holism in Literary Study.* Athens, GA: University of Georgia Press, 1988.

Cremin, Lawrence A. *American Education: The Colonial Experience 1607–1783.* New York: Harper and Row, 1970.

Day, Jeremiah and James L. Kingsley. "Report of the Yale Faculty." In *Foundations of Education in America: An Anthology of Major Thoughts and Significant Actions.* Edited by James William Noll and Samuel P. Kelly. New York: Harper and Row, 1970.

Derrida, Jacques. "The Politics of Friendship." *Journal of Philosophy* 85 (November 1988): 632–44.

D'Souza, Dinesh. *Illiberal Education: The Politics of Race and Sex on Campus.* New York: Free Press, 1991.

DuBrul, Ernest L. "Whatever Happened to the Great Books of Science?" *Gallatin Review* 10 (Winter 1990–91): 68–78.

Duran, Jane. *Toward A Feminist Epistemology.* Totowa, NJ: Rowman and Littlefield, 1986.

Eagleton, Terry. *Literary Theory: An Introduction.* Minneapolis: University of Minnesota Press, 1983.

Erickson, Peter. "Rather than Reject a Common Culture Multiculturalism Advocates a More Complicated Route by Which to Achieve It." *Chronicle of Higher Education* (June 26, 1991).

Fanon, Frantz. *The Wretched of the Earth.* Translated by Constance Farrington. New York: Grove Press, 1963.

Finn, Chester E., Jr. "A Truce in the Curricular Wars?" *National Forum* 69 (Summer 1989): 16–18.

Fish, Stanley. "Canon Busting: The Basic Issues." *National Forum* 69 (Summer 1989): 13–15.

———. *Is There a Text in This Class? The Authority of Interpretive Communities.* Cambridge, MA: Harvard University Press, 1980.

Fox-Genovese, Elizabeth. "The Feminist Challenge to the Canon." *National Forum* 69 (Summer 1989): 32–34.

———. "Gender, Race, Class, Canon." *Salmagundi* 72 (Fall 1986): 131–43.

Franklin, Benjamin. "Proposals Relating to the Education of Youth in Pensilvanie, 1749." In *The Writings of Benjamin Franklin*, vol. 2. New York: Haskell House Publishers, 1970.

Gardner, John. *On Moral Fiction*. New York: Basic Books, 1978.

Gates, Henry Louis, Jr. *Loose Canons: Notes on the Culture Wars*. New York: Oxford University Press, 1992.

Gilbert, Sandra M. and Susan Gubar. *The Madwoman in the Attic: The Woman Writer and the Nineteenth Century Literary Imagination*. New Haven: Yale University Press, 1979.

Gilligan, Carol. *In a Different Voice: Psychological Theory and Women's Development*. Cambridge: Harvard University Press, 1982.

Giroux, Henry and Harvey J. Kaye. "The Liberal Arts Must Be Reformed to Serve Democratic Ends." *Chronicle of Higher Education* (March 29, 1989).

Good, H. G. *A History of Western Education*. New York: Macmillan, 1960.

Gorak, Jan. *The Making of the Modern Canon: Genesis and Crisis of a Literary Idea.* Atlantic Heights, NJ: Athlone, 1991.

Graff, Gerald. *Beyond the Culture Wars: How Teaching the Conflicts Can Revitalize American Education*. New York: W. W. Norton, 1992.

———. "Conflicts Over the Curriculum Are Here to Stay: They Should Be Made Educationally Productive." *Chronicle of Higher Education* (February 17, 1988).

———. *Literature Against Itself: Literary Ideas in Modern Society*. Chicago: University of Chicago Press, 1979.

———. *Professing Literature: An Institutional History*. Chicago: University of Chicago Press, 1989.

———. "What Has Literary Theory Wrought?" *Chronicle of Higher Education* (February 12, 1992).

Graff, Gerald and William E. Cain. "Peace Plan for the Canon Wars." *National Forum* 69 (Summer 1989): 7–9.

The Great Conversation: A Reader's Guide to the Great Books of the Western World. Chicago: Encyclopedia Britannica, 1952, 1990.

Haack, Susan. "Knowledge and Propaganda: Reflections of an Old Feminist." *Partisan Review* 60 (1993): 556–64.

Howe, Irving. "The Value of the Canon." *New Republic* (February 18, 1991): 40–47.

Iannone, Carol. "Feminism vs. Literature." *Commentary* (July 1988): 49–53.

Jacoby, Russell. *Dogmatic Wisdom: How the Culture Wars Divert Education and Distract America.* New York: Doubleday, 1994.

Jaeger, Werner. *Paideia: The Ideals of Greek Culture,* 3 vols. New York: Oxford University Press, 1939.

"The Junior Great Books Reading and Discussion Program." Brochure from the Great Books Foundation, Chicago.

Kampf, Louis and Paul Lauter, eds. *The Politics of Literature: Dissenting Essays on the Teaching of English.* New York: Random House, 1970.

Kates, Gary. "The Classics of Western Civilization Do Not Belong to Conservatives Alone." *Chronicle of Higher Education* (July 5, 1989).

Kelly, Christopher. "Authors, Authority, and the University Curriculum." *Gallatin Review* 10 (Winter 1990–91): 93–106.

Kimball, Bruce. *Orators and Philosophers: A History of the Idea of Liberal Education.* New York: Teachers College Press, 1986.

Kimball, Roger. *Tenured Radicals: How Politics Has Corrupted Our Higher Education.* New York: Harper and Row, 1990.

Knowles, David. *The Evolution of Medieval Thought.* New York: Random House, 1962.

Knox, Bernard. *The Oldest Dead White European Males.* New York: W. W. Norton, 1993.

Krieger, Murray. *The Institution of Theory.* Baltimore, MD: Johns Hopkins University Press, 1994.

"Legislation for the Area One Requirement: Cultures, Ideas, and Values (CIV)," adopted by the Faculty Senate of Stanford University, March 1988.

Levine, George, et al. *Speaking for the Humanities.* American Council of Learned Societies Occasional Paper No. 7, 1989.

Lucas, Christopher. *Our Western Educational Heritage.* New York: Macmillan, 1972.

Mansfield, Harvey C., Jr. "Democracy and the Great Books." *New Republic* (April 4, 1988): 33–37.

Marrou, H. I. *A History of Education in Antiquity.* New York: Mentor, 1964.

Martin, Jerry L. "The Postmodern Argument Reconsidered." *Partisan Review* 60 (1993): 638–54.

Massey, Donna B. "The Art is in the Balancing: Canon Expansion in *The Norton Anthology of American Literature.*" Washington, DC: U.S. Department of Education, ERIC Report.

McArthur, Benjamin. "The War of the Great Books." *American Heritage* 40 (February 1989): 57–69.

McCarthy, Thomas. *Ideals and Illusions: On Reconstruction and Deconstruction in Contemporary Critical Theory.* Cambridge, MA: MIT Press, 1991.

Meynell, Hugo. "Fish Fingered: Anatomy of a Deconstructionist." *Journal of Aesthetic Education* 23 (Summer 1989): 5–15.

Morrisey, Will. "Ideology and Literary Studies: PMLA 1930–1990." *Academic Questions* (Winter 1992–93): 54–66.

Oakeshott, Michael. *The Voice of Liberal Learning: Michael Oakeshott on Education.* New Haven: Yale University Press, 1989.

Ortega y Gasset, Jose. *Mission of the University.* Translated and edited by Howard Lee Nostrand. New Brunswick, NJ: Transaction Publishers, 1992.

Peterman, James F., and D. E. Richardson. "A Rally for the Academic Left." *Sewanee Review* (Fall 1989): 622–27.

Rashdall, Hastings. *The Universities of Europe in the Middle Ages,* 3 vols. London: Oxford University Press, 1936.

Ravitch, Diane. "Multiculturalism Yes, Particularism No." *Chronicle of Higher Education* (October 24, 1990).

Ridder-Simoens, Hilde de, ed. *Universities in the Middle Ages.* New York: Cambridge University Press, 1992.

Rorty, Richard. "That Old Time Philosophy." *New Republic* (April 4, 1988): 28–33.

Said, Edward. *Orientalism.* New York: Vintage, 1979.

Scholes, Robert. "Aiming a Canon at the Curriculum." *Salmagundi* 72 (Fall 1986): 101–17.

———. *Textual Power.* New Haven: Yale University Press, 1985.

Scholes, Robert, Nancy R. Comley, and Gregory Ulmer. *Textbook: An Introduction to Literary Language.* New York: St. Martin's Press, 1988.

Searle, John R. "Is There a Crisis in American Higher Education?" *Partisan Review* 60 (1993): 693–709.

———. "The Storm Over the University." *New York Review of Books* (December 6, 1990).

Simonson, Rick and Scott Walker. *The Graywolf Annual Five: Multicultural Literacy.* St. Paul, MN: Graywolf Press, 1988.

Smith, Barbara Herrnstein. *Contingencies of Value: Alternative Perspectives for Critical Theory.* Cambridge, MA: Harvard University Press, 1988.

Spivak, Gayatri Chakravorty. *In Other Worlds: Essays in Cultural Politics.* London: Methuen, 1987.

Stanford, Michael. "The Stanford Library." *New Republic* (October 2, 1989): 18–20.

Strauss, Leo. "What is Liberal Education?" In *An Introduction to Political Philosophy: Ten Essays By Leo Strauss.* Detroit: Wayne State University Press, 1989.

Sullivan, William. "The 'Norton Anthology' and the Canon of English Literature." Washington, DC: U.S. Department of Education, ERIC Report.

Swift, Jonathan. "A Full and True Account of the Battel Between the Antient and Modern Books in St. James Library." In *Gulliver's Travels and Other Writings.* New York: Bantam Books, 1962.

Taylor, Charles. *Multiculturalism and "The Politics of Recognition."* Princeton: Princeton University Press, 1992.

Tompkins, Jane. *Sensational Designs: The Cultural Work of American Fiction, 1790–1860*. New York: Oxford University Press, 1985.

Von Halberg, Robert, ed. *Canons*. Chicago: University of Chicago Press, 1983.

Waddell, Helen. *The Wandering Scholars*. New York: Houghton Mifflin, 1927.

Watts, Steven. "Academia's Leftists Are Something of a Fraud." *Chronicle of Higher Education* (April 29, 1992).

Weinsheimer, Joel. *Philosophical Hermeneutics and Literary Theory*. New Haven: Yale University Press, 1991.

Westphal, Merold. "The Canon as Flexible, Normative Fact." *Monist* 76 (October 1993): 436–49.

"Who Needs Great Works?" *Harper's* (September 1989): 43–52.

Yates, Steven. "Multiculturalism and Epistemology." *Public Affairs Quarterly* (1993): 435–56.

Zingg, Paul J. "Quality in the Curriculum: The Renewed Search for Coherence and Unity." *Journal of General Education* 39 (1987): 173–92.

INDEX